PRAISE F(

"I'm not an expert in real estate; I'm not an expert in finance, but I know something about recognizing a fresh voice with something important to say. Chris Hurn has built a fast-growing, entrepreneurial company by helping other entrepreneurs finance their dreams and build long-term wealth. There's nothing more powerful in business than a combination of smart money and big ideas. Chris Hurn is a master of both, and his book will help your company get bigger faster."

—**WILLIAM C. TAYLOR,** Cofounder of *Fast Company* magazine and bestselling author of *Practically Radical*

"Chris Hurn is a small business owner writing and providing commercial real estate solutions for entrepreneurs and fellow business owners like you. Chris takes his area of expertise for helping build wealth through commercial property ownership and offers it generously in a well-organized and empowering way. His insights on the intricacies of small business loans, his cache of business development resources, and the case studies of his clients make this book an invaluable resource for those who want to convert leases and rent payments into a very powerful business asset. Thanks for adeptly addressing a subject all too long neglected in business publishing."

—**JOSEPH MICHELLI, PH.D.,** leadership and customer experience consultant, speaker, and *New York Times* #1 bestselling author of books such as *The Starbucks Experience*, *The Zappos Experience*, and *The New Gold Standard*

"Chris is a brilliant expert in an area of far-too-often neglected financial opportunity for just about every kind of business owner; creating wealth for themselves by owning commercial property in which their business is housed, instead of creating wealth for a landlord. In a lifetime, most business owners hand over millions of dollars to other property owners that could have accumulated for their own retirement. On a broader note, I often speak of business owners' single-minded obsession with income and lack of attention to equity. This book fits into that vital discussion."

—**DAN S. KENNEDY,** author of *No B.S. Business Success in the New Economy* and *No B.S. Wealth Attraction in the New Economy*

"It's often said that the most surefire way to become wealthy is to buy good real estate and hold it for 100 years. If you don't want to wait that long, read this book. I wish I'd had it when I went into business."

— **Norm Brodsky**, founder of CitiStorage, columnist for *Inc.* magazine, and author of *Street Smarts: An All-Purpose Tool Kit for Entrepreneurs*

"As an entrepreneur, it is not enough to merely build a *business*. We must also build wealth. In this book, Chris Hurn reveals his insider strategies and step-by-step tactics for creating our lifelong fortune. Plenty of books describe how entrepreneurs can create more ideas or happier employees. However, no other business book outlines in such detail and with such authority how to actually develop the wealth behind the business."

—**Sally Hogshead**, creator of HowToFascinate.com and bestselling author of *Fascinate: Your 7 Triggers to Persuasion and Captivation*

"When it comes to creating wealth, there are definitely secrets, shortcuts and unconventional strategies out there that most business owners don't know about. Chris Hurn knows them all. Heck, he's pioneered a few of them. This book gives you a peek inside and shows you how to use these strategies to build your fortune."

—**Jimmy Vee and Travis Miller**, best-selling authors of *Gravitational Marketing: The Science of Attracting Customers*

"Chris Hurn is a commercial property genius. He and I have been friends for years and over the course of our friendship, he continually demonstrates a deep and profound knowledge on how to finance suitable and appropriate commercial property acquisitions for the small business owner. Through his skill set, he has helped hundreds of small business owners transition from being renters to becoming commercial property owners and investors in quality real estate. It's refreshing to finally see someone truly help small business owners as they grow and provide employment for their communities. Two thumbs up!"

— **Chris Tomshack** DC, CEO of HealthSource Chiropractic (ranked the top overall newer franchise in America by *Entrepreneur* magazine, the #1 franchise in health services by *Entrepreneur* magazine four years in a row, and the fastest-growing franchise in America by *Franchise Times* two years in a row)

"Chris takes a decidedly off-centered approach to entrepreneurship, which I think will have broad appeal to business-minded readers. Every business owner looking to get to the proverbial 'next level' ought to read this book to learn one of the best ways to create wealth, while simultaneously growing your business. I should know, as my company has used a good number of the approaches championed here on our path of strong growth in a highly competitive industry."

—SAM CALAGIONE, President and Founder of Dogfish Head Brewery

"This book will solve for you many of the mysteries surrounding how certain highly successful business owners have built wealth for themselves with surprising ease. If you are an entrepreneur who wants to do something simple, to the point, and satisfying in order to grow your net worth, you have found the perfect book. It has the rare virtue of being simple, without being simplistic. Chris understands and practices what he preaches so well that he can lay it out in a deceptively straightforward, intuitive, and general manner at first. He then takes you gradually to a deeper and deeper understanding of what matters most; a step-by-step process that you might well look back upon as central to the wealth you accumulate throughout your career."

—ERIC ABRAHAMSON, Hughie E. Mills Professor of Business Management at Columbia Business School and author of *A Perfect Mess*

"Small business has no better friend than Chris Hurn, and he demonstrates it yet again in this insightful book. It's an invaluable guide to a crucial, but often overlooked, aspect of building a business."

—BO BURLINGHAM, editor-at-large of *Inc.* magazine and author of *Small Giants: Companies That Choose to Be Great Instead of Big*

"I have used the SBA 504 program three times, and I can tell you why it is so powerful: the magic of compound interest combined with the stability of being your own tenant. Much of the risk in real estate is from the possibility of being left with an empty building, so renting to your own business provides a tremendous advantage, and since there is only a 10 percent down payment involved, the return on investment (ROI) is very high, likely in the 15–20 percent range, without the typical risks associated with that high of a return. Do this for twenty years and you end up with a very nice nest egg. I have used Chris's methodology three times, and was able to both expand my business and add another revenue stream that builds over the years. In the long run, the result is a dramatically improved net worth."

—JAY GOLTZ, Lead Small Business Blogger for the *New York Times*, author of *The Street Smart Entrepreneur*, and owner of five Chicago businesses

"This book teaches small business owners how to create wealth for themselves while growing their businesses. It's one of the ultimate advantages underdogs (small businesses) have over their big business brethren. Chris unrolls the blueprints here for making your dreams come true."

— DAVID MOREY, author of *The Underdog Advantage* and CEO of DMG, Inc.

"If you've ever considered buying the real estate on and in which you do business, this book is a great how-to guide, filled with a plethora of practical tips that can help you make it happen and make you money in the process. If you haven't considered buying, this book might well change your mind!"

— ARI WEINZWEIG, Cofounder of Zingerman's Community of Businesses and author of *Zingerman's Guide to Good Eating*

"If you want to learn hands-on strategies for your own financial freedom, then you should devour this book."

—T. HARV EKER, author of the *New York Times* #1 bestseller *Secrets of the Millionaire Mind*

"This book is a must-read for today's Main Street entrepreneur. He's a champion of America's small business owners and in this book, he literally pulls back the curtain and shows you what is truly possible by following his advice."

— BOB COLEMAN, Founder of Coleman Publishing (the leading media authority in small business lending) and author of *Money Money Everywhere, But Not a Drop for Main Street*

"If you are a successful entrepreneur and you wish to build your business and your wealth, there is powerful information in this book for you. Chris Hurn reveals the secrets and techniques to add another pillar of stability and growth to your business. What Chris teaches is the next – and often most critical – step in the evolution of your business."

— **ROB BERKLEY,** Master Certified Coach, Executive Coach, and Cofounder of www.visionday.com

THE
ENTREPRENEUR'S
SECRET
TO
CREATING
WEALTH

THE
ENTREPRENEUR'S
SECRET
TO
CREATING
WEALTH

How the Smartest Business Owners
Build their Fortunes

CHRIS HURN

*A*dvantage®

Published by Advantage, Charleston, South Carolina.
Member of Advantage Media Group.

ADVANTAGE is a registered trademark and the Advantage colophon is a trademark of Advantage Media Group, Inc.

Printed in the United States of America.

ISBN: 978-1-59932-315-2
LCCN: 2012949210

This publication is designed to provide accurate and authoritative information in regard to the subject matter covered. It is sold with the understanding that the publisher is not engaged in rendering legal, accounting, or other professional services. If legal advice or other expert assistance is required, the services of a competent professional person should be sought.

Advantage Media Group is proud to be a part of the Tree Neutral® program. Tree Neutral offsets the number of trees consumed in the production and printing of this book by taking proactive steps such as planting trees in direct proportion to the number of trees used to print books. To learn more about Tree Neutral, please visit www.treeneutral.com. To learn more about Advantage's commitment to being a responsible steward of the environment, please visit www.advantagefamily.com/green

Advantage Media Group is a leading publisher of business, motivation, and self-help authors. Do you have a manuscript or book idea that you would like to have considered for publication? Please visit www.advantagefamily.com or call 1.866.775.1696

*To my loving family (Shannon, Julianna, and Reilly), my
friends, and my team members at Mercantile.*

*And, to America's small business owners and entrepreneurs who are truly the key
drivers of economic progress and prosperity. I KNOW you build it, every single day.*

Table of contents

*It is not because things are difficult that we do not dare; it
is because we do not dare that they are difficult.*
—Seneca, Roman philosopher

About the Author — 15

Introduction — 19

Chapter One
Why Own Rather than Rent? — 39

Chapter Two
Getting Organized — 67

Chapter Three
Finding a Good Real Estate Broker — 93

Chapter Four
Finding a Good Lender — 115

Chapter Five
Obtaining the Best Loan — 143

Chapter Six
The SmartChoice® Alternative — 165

Chapter Seven
Exploding the Myths — 205

Conclusion — 223

Special Offer for Intrepid Readers — 227

APPENDIX A
Certified Development Companies — 229

APPENDIX B
Commercial Real Estate Brokers — 245

Other Business Books in Which I've Appeared — 249

You Can Do It — 251

Build Your Team Wisely — 265

Acknowledgements and Gratitude — 273

Investing in Our Future — 277

About the Author

"Real estate is the basis of wealth," Theodore Roosevelt once stated, and his cousin Franklin called it "about the safest investment in the world." Most business owners will tell you they would very much like to own their commercial property. It's what some call the next American dream, after owning your home and being your own boss.

But most banks require 20 to 35 percent down, and they'll rarely fix an interest rate for long. Cash flow, it's said, is the lifeblood of any small business, and many business owners can't afford to sink that much cash into a commercial property.

That's where author Chris Hurn can help you. He and Geof Longstaff founded Mercantile Capital Corp. (MCC) in late 2002 to help owners of small and mid-size businesses fulfill their dreams of commercial property ownership through smarter financing.

Hurn spent years in small business lending with several large institutions, and he came to realize how difficult it could be for small businesses to meet the capital requirements of ordinary bank financing. He also recognized the solution—a little-known and underutilized SBA program called the 504 loan—and joined with Longstaff to establish a company that would specialize in these loans.

Rebranding the SBA 504 loan as the SmartChoice® Commercial Loan, they began educating business owners and their advisors about financing options that many banks were unwilling to reveal. This loan program allows business owners to purchase commercial property with as little as 10 percent down at below-market, long-term fixed interest rates.

"I'm one of these guys who walks my talk," Hurn says. "I have one of these loans myself when I had many alternatives, so I've been in the shoes of our prospective borrowers. If I chose the SBA 504 loan for myself, that clearly demonstrates my faith in it. I've become a small business advocate over the years. I have a passion for helping entrepreneurs succeed, in the smartest way possible, and that includes creating wealth through commercial property ownership."

Mercantile Capital Corp. has since worked with scores of business owners from all over the nation to help fulfill their dreams of commercial property ownership. The company has had over 450 clients in 37 states, Puerto Rico, and the District of Columbia. As of July 2012, it has financed projects for nearly $1.1 billion worth of commercial property. It has financed commercial property for event planners, bakers, auto auction companies, cell phone refurbishers, numerous hotels and restaurants, day-care facilities for children and for adults, distribution companies, physicians' and financial planners' offices, accountants, dentists, veterinarians, website hosting companies, marketing companies—the list goes on and on.

Hurn has been featured in the *Wall Street Journal, New York Times, Los Angeles Times, Bloomberg Businessweek, Forbes, Inc.* magazine, *SmartMoney, Scotsman Guide, Franchise Times, Franchising World,* and *Restaurant Finance Monitor,* among others. Hurn has also appeared on *Fox Business News* numerous times as well as PBS's *Nightly Business Report,* to discuss small business lending in the current economic environment and has a regular column on the *Huffington Post.*

The company's accolades include being named to the *Inc.* 500/5000 list of the fastest-growing companies in America in 2009, 2008, and 2007; the *Orlando Business Journal's (OBJ)* "Best Places to Work" (2009, 2007, 2006, and 2005); the *OBJ's* "Best Small Company in Central Florida" (2007) and "Outstanding Small Business" Award (2008); and Seminole County (Florida) Regional Chamber of Commerce's "Business of the Year" (2008). Hurn was also named a Top 100 Small Business Influencer (2012); the SBA's "Financial Services Champion of the Year" (2010 and 2006); NADCO's "Banker of the Year" (2006); one of *Coleman Publishing*'s "Top 20 Most Influential People in Small Business Lending" (2008); and *Coleman Publishing*'s "Marketing Guru of the Year" (2007).

In 2008 Hurn cofounded the award-winning Kennedy's All-American Barber Club®, a chain of upscale men's barber shops from Florida to Connecticut for which he is chairman and CEO (www. KennedysBarberClub.com). At Mercantile, Hurn came to appreciate franchise business models after franchising nearly six dozen different concepts over the year. "I came across a very fragmented, mom-and-pop-type marketplace in men's grooming. And there was a huge opportunity to bring back the civilized gentleman barber shop of old and to update it with such things as a predominantly membership-based business, modern products, hand-selected music, and so on. We actually have a patent pending on our membership business model too. Kennedy's is what I consider to be a necessity-based business, and it has quite the potential to grow across the country."

As the CEO of Mercantile, Hurn not only serves on its board but is also on the board of the National Association of Premier Lenders (NAPL), the National Federation of Independent Business (NFIB) Florida Leadership Council, and is active with the International Franchise Association (IFA) and the Florida Bankers Association (FBA).

Hurn lives in a northeast suburb of Orlando called Lake Mary (Heathrow) with his wife, Shannon, two children, and two dogs. "I've got four babies," Hurn says. "I've got an eleven-year-old daughter, a nine-year-old son, Mercantile, and Kennedy's. I spend most of my time on those four babies. I do get one reprieve: I'm a huge soccer fan, so once the work is done and the family is in bed, I may get to watch the soccer channel for half an hour most nights. I even catch a whole game from time to time, and I also play on the over-forty Lake Mary Football Club team, but I enjoy plenty of other sports too. You can't live in the South and not support college football."

CONTACT INFORMATION:

Mercantile Capital Corporation
60 North Court Avenue, Suite #200
Orlando, FL 32801
Phone: 407-786-5040
Toll Free: 1-866-622-4504
Fax: 407-682-1632

Visit www.504Experts.com to learn more about Mercantile, read Chris' blog, and connect with them on YouTube, Facebook, Twitter, LinkedIn, and Google Plus. You can also sign up to get periodic updates on all things related to smarter, small-business, commercial real estate financing, as well as an occasional bit of lighthearted nonsense. Rest assured, they only send content written by Chris to folks on their email list – so zero spam – and they'll never give your information to anyone else. Again, sign up at www.504Experts.com or by sending an email to info@mercantilecc.com indicating you'd like to be added to the Mercantile mailing list.

Introduction

Entrepreneurship is living a few years of your life like most people won't,
so that you can spend the rest of your life like most people can't.
—ANONYMOUS

Some people dream of great accomplishments while others stay awake and do them.
—ANONYMOUS

I can remember the moment when the dots connected in my head. I was thirteen years old and helping my mother study to take her real estate license exam when I realized something that would change the course of my life.

I grew up outside Peoria, Illinois, raised by my mother, Suzanne, a single parent. She was a chocolatier. People in downstate Illinois are still familiar with her and her company, which was called Sweet Tooth Limited and operated from our home. I helped her in that business even as a little boy. It was one of my first experiences in entrepreneurship and selling.

I also had my own business, which I started when I was eight. I cut grass and raked leaves and shoveled snow for neighbors in our little town of Bartonville, which was near a Caterpillar plant and associated industries but not much else except rural Midwest farmland.

Once, some buddies and I actually imagined ourselves as farmers of a sort. We were convinced my neighbor was growing wild marijuana in her yard, as if we knew what it was, and fancied ourselves as tough potential drug dealers. It turned out my neighbor was growing hemp. I'm glad we "tested" our potential product first (and realized our error). This wasn't exactly my finest idea to date, even though it's now become a cliché: the drug dealer turned budding entrepreneur. So it was back to work for me at McDonald's (the only place in town that would hire a fourteen-year-old) and dreaming of faraway places and future profits.

My mother at one point decided to become a real estate agent, and I would quiz her on the questions in her workbooks. We did that for weeks and weeks, and I found that it was vastly different from many things that I was learning in high school, where you're trying to memorize all those dates in history and how to conjugate verbs. What I was reading to my mother seemed far more useful.

We talked, she and I, about how real estate creates wealth for people, how once you move out of an apartment and buy a house, you actually have something of value that probably is going to appreciate over time. You're no longer throwing your money away on rent. I could see that clearly at thirteen, and the concept stuck with me.

My mother was actively pursuing something that would advance her further into the business world. I admire that kind of initiative. She went on to work as a real estate agent for a decade and kept her chocolatier business. She still makes candies to this day, though not to the same extent.

What I observed as a child was my mother raising two boys and having multiple jobs. Her example encouraged me to do the same: working while maintaining my academics, extracurriculars, sports, and all the rest of life's demands and interests. Sadly, that work ethic seems to be lacking in our culture these days, but if you are a small business owner and/or entrepreneur, you can relate to its fundamental importance.

The Lightbulb Moment

You also likely can relate to this: You've been in business for several years, paying a monthly lease and possibly watching it rise regularly, and you wake up one morning with the realization that you are throwing your hard-earned money away. You likely felt the same way when you moved from an apartment to a house, and now it dawns on you that the principle holds true for ownership of commercial property.

That's the point when you too have connected those dots. I understand that, and that's why I got into small business lending. I founded Mercantile Capital Corporation because I can relate to the typical small business person. I am one. I know what it's like to have to meet payroll. I understand the daily issues and problems—what I call having your hair on fire—and I have spent many days putting out fires (there's literally an old-fashioned fire chief's helmet in my office, which belonged to my great-grandfather). It was natural for me to pick this particular niche of financing.

Whether you're a busy physician, restaurateur, or day-care provider, this book will show you how to maximize your opportunity to build wealth through owning commercial property. Before I wrote this book, I researched this subject to see if anyone else had written about it. No one had written a book just for business owners and their advisors. There's a lot to consider before taking the plunge and purchasing your property, so I'm going to give you some insider tips in this book on how to do it right.

I will tell you more about a little-known and still underused financing tool (even though it's been around for nearly three decades) that will help you make your investment count. We specialize in loans through the SBA's 504 program, which I often describe as the agency's best-kept secret and which I know through experience will serve you best. We call it the SmartChoice® Commercial Loan, and it's one your banker may well overlook, but it's one you need as you pursue your dream of growing your wealth through commercial real estate. (Note: I use the terms *SBA 504, 504,* and *SmartChoice*® Commercial Loan interchangeably throughout this book.)

It's much like the American dream of moving out of an apartment and buying your own home, owning your own castle. I've extended that logic to small-business owners. You don't have to just lease a facility for the next twenty years and throw your money away on rent. This can be another great wealth creation enhancement for you.

I've read a study that claimed most small business owners in America have not saved a dime for their retirement. If you or those you advise apply my simple concepts here, the ownership of commercial property can become a great retirement strategy. Whether you someday still own a business, sell it, or close it down, you will still probably retain possession of the commercial property if you avail yourself of what I teach. You can become somebody else's landlord and that can provide a nice passive income stream well into your retirement. Doing this may be your biggest and most important investment ever, so it's critical you do this right.

Foundations of a Career

Bartonville was an interesting place to grow up, but I found it a less interesting place to stick around: I left at age seventeen and only go back to visit my mother and brother occasionally.

After high school I went to the big city, Chicago, for my undergraduate degree at Loyola University, Chicago. I actually earned two bachelor's degrees—*magna cum laude* in both of them—in four years. From there I went to the University of Pennsylvania in Philadelphia.

I'd been the first in my family to go to college, and now I found myself in the Ivy League. I received my master's there from the Fels Institute, which was part of the Wharton School of Business at that time. My focus was more on public policy and finance as opposed to just purely on business.

From there I moved to Washington, DC. I thought I would work in government and politics. I did, for a while, but who can live on such pay? At one point I turned down a job from Ari Fleischer, a congressional aide who later became President George W. Bush's press secretary. It was for about $18,000 a year. That's why some have called Capitol Hill the "last plantation." A young person can't survive there very well unless he or she has, say, a wealthy uncle or a trust fund for support. I had neither.

So there I was with two bachelor's degrees and a master's degree from an Ivy League school, and I humbly took my very first job with a temp service. I was promoted quickly into a position in sales and marketing. The work on Capitol Hill is about selling concepts and ideas. That's essentially what politics is. I realized that didn't pay as well as selling an *actual* product or service. There are other correlations there as well, Washington versus the real world, but that's another discussion entirely.

That temp job right out of grad school turned out to be with a high-tech startup, which I joined before it was fashionable to do so. It was the country's first digital wireless provider, American Personal Communications, which evolved into Sprint's national wireless network. It was very fast growing, and within a couple of years I had numerous recruiters calling since I was one of the company's top salespeople. One of the offers I received was from GE Capital, to work with small businesses. I liked the thought of that. I could work with small businesses, financing them, whether they were doing commercial real estate purchases, equipment purchases, business acquisitions, equipment leases, looking for startup capital, and so forth. I found all that to be too intriguing to turn down.

About the same time, I was accepted into Georgetown Law School. I was thinking I might eventually want to become an attorney. That seed was planted in my head when I was thirteen. My father hadn't been in my life much since I was around nine years old, and my parents finally got divorced when I was thirteen. It was on the evening of my grade school graduation, at which I was the master of ceremonies, that my mother told me she and my father were divorcing, and they did so shortly thereafter. I remember one of their lawyers saying, "Wow, I don't think I've met a kid your age who is as level-headed and as conversant in things as you are. You'd make a fabulous litigator someday."

That got me to thinking, perhaps unfortunately. I entered the Georgetown Law School night program. It would take four years to earn my JD degree. During the day, I wanted to stay in the business world. My cost-benefit analysis led me to turn down a full ride at the University of Illinois' Law School. I didn't want a sabbatical from earning while learning.

I would leave my condo at six in the morning and go to the gym to work out. I needed to prime myself with energy. Then I'd go to my day job till 5:30 p.m. or so, take the Metro downtown, and walk over to attend Georgetown Law. I'd see the Capitol dome in the distance—a great sight at night—as I hustled to class. Then, back on the Metro and home around 10:30 p.m. in time to collapse, sleep awhile, and do it all over the next day. There was little time for studying. There was, however, some time for romance: I got married about that same time to the love of my life.

So, after a year at Georgetown Law, I made the tough decision to leave—my $100,000 decision as I call it now, since I had a load of student loans, but the opportunity cost of losing time in the business world would have been even greater, and I would have racked up about $100,000 more in student loans had I stayed on that path.

When I was in college, between my first year and sophomore year, I worked in the General Assembly in Springfield, Illinois. I was also an intern for one semester for U.S. Senator Paul Simon of Illinois. I worked on a number of different campaigns over the years, congressional, senatorial, and state representative. For a little while, before I started full-time work, I even did some work raising money for senatorial campaigns. I wrote some congressional testimony once for another internship, which was more of a business-focused interest group (the PENJERDEL Council).

That experience too was good preparation for my career today. I go to Capitol Hill two to three times a year to lobby, making sure people are aware of the SBA 504 program and keep supporting it. The SBA is a political entity, though it now has support from both sides of the aisle, at least most of the time. I'm sure at some point I'll do something more political, but for the time being, it doesn't pay that well considering all the headaches and gridlock incumbent in the job. Being an entrepreneur, while not the easiest thing in the world, certainly seems more rewarding.

When I was working at GE Capital, the SBA 504 program was one of the product lines we offered. To this day I use a lot of what I learned about managerial and leadership skills from GE. It was a great training ground for that sort of thing. GE had a big focus on SBA 504 loans, and it was one of the larger small-business lenders, a nonbank small-business lender, at that time. So I just fell into it. It was a natural fit for my interests.

Even now, GE is a massive conglomerate with many seemingly disparate entities: GE Plastics, GE Capital, GE Rail, GE Nuclear. It has owned NBC and theme parks and many other entities that don't seem to have a lot to do with one another. GE Capital tried to connect all these interests: If you needed to order aircraft engines or twenty tons of plastic pellets, GE Capital would help get you the financing. Or if you were a purchaser from GE Industrial, maybe you needed some accounts receivable (AR) financing or a line of credit.

So I worked for this massive company, which was headed by the highly regarded Jack Welch and focused on financing small and mid-size companies effectively. It used the SBA lending programs because they had some advantages not just for the borrowers but also for the lender—that is, it got a government guarantee, which of course reduced the risk to GE Capital.

Yet those who worked in the GE industries—plastics, or NBC, or making aircraft engines or building power plants—specialized in their own world within this huge company. All these industrial businesses spun off cash that could then be put back to use through the Capital channel. In other words, GE would generate cash from its industrial businesses, which would be pushed back out through the capital side of the company.

All that made a big impression on me, in addition to the managerial and leadership skills that I was learning at GE. I came to see that there was something to be said for not being all things to all people and really focusing. The problem with the GE strategy under Jack Welch was that the divisions became systems of people doing their own thing, seemingly independent of the large whole. Despite the rhetoric of "focus," how could GE be focused with literally hundreds of departments? The antidote, I thought, was to try to be the best at only one thing.

I believe the ability to say no to somebody—"No, that doesn't fit our core competency"—is rather profound in terms of enhancing your credibility, furthering your positioning, getting your team back on the plan, and so forth. It's something that you don't see a lot of people do. Everybody is really in sales, but if something is just a little bit outside the company's core competency, the natural inclination of any salesperson is to say, "Yeah, we can probably do that," and then it becomes a stretch to make it happen.

There are fairly rigid rules regarding SBA loans. At the time, I felt GE preferred the SBA 504 loan because of the structure and the risk mitigation that it received, and I felt that GE was one of the few places that actually liked to do the 504. Everybody else at that time, and still to this day, likes to lead with a better-known SBA product called the 7(a) loan. The 504 has many more advantageous elements to it for small business owners and for the marketplace than the 7(a), yet nobody other than GE at that time was promoting it.

I resolved to spread the word about the 504 when I cofounded Mercantile Capital Corp. in late 2002. I'd also been the CFO for the second largest commercial real estate brokerage firm in Orlando, NAI Realvest Partners. I joined NAI in late 2001, nearly in conjunction with starting Mercantile.

Besides GE Capital, my resume would show I had worked for Heller Financial, which was later bought by GE Capital, and that I was a management consultant for a number of years, first at Marsh & McLennan Companies (MMC) and then with American Management Services, and in those roles I was responsible for basically four areas: operational consulting, organizational consulting, strategic and marketing consulting, and financial consulting for small to mid-size companies. I used to travel daily. It's basically a young person's game, and once my daughter was born, I needed to slow that down a bit.

In launching Mercantile, I felt it would be a terrific business proposition to be the world's best specialist in an underutilized product. Consider what happened recently with big banks and Wall Street investment companies that tried to be all things to all people. It blew up on them: they were jacks of all trades, masters of none. It was like a guy opening his trench coat hoping something he's peddling on one side or the other might interest you. It's in business people's DNA to try to do whatever the prospect wants, but it's often a losing proposition that in time dilutes them and hurts their positioning. I wanted to avoid that.

When I had the idea of starting Mercantile, cofounder Geof Longstaff and I went to a number of the bankers in town with whom we were pretty close to see if they wanted to join forces with us. Most responded with something like this: "Let me get this straight. Number one, you're going to do primarily, if not exclusively, one loan product, right?" I said yes. It came across as ridiculous because they instinctively wanted to do it all, which is what consultants and business-school types might liken to "vertical integration." We see this to this day with many bankers, but even if they could accept our narrow business focus, they had another question: "And number two, you're going to make it a government-guaranteed loan product, right?" I said, "Yes." And that's usually when they'd start laughing and walk away shaking their head in disbelief.

Several of those bankers now are unemployed or have left the field altogether. I don't want to relish in their failure, but I think I was a bit ahead of my time in the boutique approach to creating a specialty finance company. It really hadn't been done much that way before. For years, people thought we were crazy to refuse business that did not fit within our tight definitions, but we continued to do so.

Recently, I spoke on two consecutive days at a sales and marketing event for small-business lending professionals. I pointed out that since starting our company, we had spent over $4 million just marketing the SBA 504 product. Even the giant banks, the household names such as Wells Fargo, Bank of America, and JPMorgan Chase, probably haven't spent $4 million in the last eight years just to promote the 504 loan, but, because of our leadership in promoting this product, we are now acknowledged as the industry's experts throughout the country.

Back when I started Mercantile, I did some deep analysis of lending programs for small businesses. I was looking for a population base that I could compare to Central Florida's, where I originally expected to do all my business with 504 loans. I found that Utah was a fit in size and number of small businesses—the entire state of Utah, that is. In the year 2000, according to the latest figures I had, Utah's population was roughly the same as what I expected to be our footprint in Central Florida. I thought I was going to lend money in the six- or seven-county region around Orlando. The number of small businesses in the region at the time also correlated well to Utah's. However, I discovered that seven times the number of SBA 504 loans had been done in the entire state of Utah as compared to the metro Orlando area, even as far up as Jacksonville. Like a classic entrepreneur, I saw this massive opportunity, and that's what we jumped on.

To this day, the West Coast is a much bigger proponent and adopter of the 504 program than the East Coast. The farther east you go from California, the less people seem to know about the 504, whether lenders, mortgage brokers, real estate brokers, accountants, or real estate attorneys. I don't really know why that is, but if a lot of West Coast trends are questionable at best, this one happens to be quite good. In California the small business marketplace is a tremendous adopter of the 504. To this day, California typically accounts for about 30 to 35 percent of all the 504 loans done in America.

My company has disrupted that dramatically, particularly in Florida where we started, but we're not just an Orlando-based lender anymore. Our territory has expanded greatly. Within a few years we were working with prospects all around the country, and today, our own backyard represents less than 10 percent of the total deals that we close in a given year.

A Closer Look at SBA Loans

The SBA is an agency of the federal government and the only one that is dedicated exclusively to America's small businesses. It was started in the mid-1950s, during the Eisenhower administration. During the Clinton administration, the SBA administrator was a cabinet member and still should be, I believe, considering that statistics show small businesses account for about half the private sector payroll in this country and represent about half the gross domestic product. (As I was writing this book, President Obama elevated the SBA administrator to his cabinet.)

The SBA is known primarily for two loan programs: the 7(a) and the 504. The former predates the latter by quite some time. The 504 is only about thirty years old. The 7(a) has a greater range of use of proceeds; you can do more with those loans. You can use them to finance a business acquisition. In this country, very little small-business acquisition financing is done through conventional banks. It's almost exclusively done with the SBA 7(a) or seller financing. You can do partner buyouts with the 7(a); you can finance commercial real estate; you can finance equipment; you can finance inventory and receivables (working capital financing); you can do startup financing—quite a variety of uses.

In contrast, the 504 is exclusively used for hard assets, and by that I mean commercial real estate and heavy equipment/machinery, in addition to some "soft" costs related to financing your project. That's it. Congress did recently open a temporary window of opportunity, as an allowable use of SBA 504 funds, to include, for the first time, the *refinancing* of commercial real estate with some working capital included.

There are two other crucial differences between the SBA loan programs that we'll be discussing in this book. First, the 7(a) mostly has a floating interest rate structure, while the 504 is generally fixed. Second, the 7(a) is considered a fully collateralized loan program. That's where the SBA has gotten some flak over the years: entrepreneurs expect they'll have to pledge their homes, get life insurance, and let the bank put a lien on their receivables and inventory, which will get in the way of a line of credit, and on and on. You don't have that with a 504: you're only generally collateralizing what you're financing, and that's it. So if you're buying a building, it's just the building that has a lien against it. If you're buying heavy equipment, it's just the heavy equipment.

The SBA has certainly gotten some black eyes over the years. I would argue it's almost exclusively a result of the 7(a) program and some of the things that have happened in that program politically over the years in terms of needing additional appropriations from Congress and other such matters.

Until the Great Recession, the 7(a) was also a zero-subsidy program like the 504, which had been a zero-subsidy program for almost twenty-five years, meaning that the fees borrowers and lenders pay effectively go into an "insurance pool" that covers losses in the program. A very small subsidy has been needed in the past couple of years since the real estate bubble burst, but I expect 504 to get back to its historical zero-subsidy nature soon. In fact, in the last two fiscal years of the George W. Bush administration, these fees created a surplus that was then diverted elsewhere, probably into Treasury's "black hole."

But the bottom line is that these programs have been very successful. I consider these two SBA programs some of the most successful economic programs ever created by our government. They really are a public-private partnership, the kind that taxpayers and voters tend to appreciate. These programs are growing the big businesses of tomorrow. They're growing jobs. They are supporting the job creators of today and into the future.

Hundreds of billions of dollars of SBA-supported funding has been deployed over the decades to help grow small businesses into the big businesses of the future. Apple, Columbia Sportswear, FedEx, Gymboree, Intel, Nike, Outback Steakhouse, Under Armour, Dell, Yankee Candle, and many, many others were once financed with SBA programs. And statistics clearly show that between 60 percent and 80 percent of the net job creation in this country comes from those very small businesses.

There is a host of reasons to be supportive of the SBA, and as people come to understand more about what it does, fewer will think it's just another government handout program. The SBA doesn't lend money. It relies upon private-sector lenders like us to deploy the funds. The government merely puts a guarantee on a portion of the funds, which is paid for (with fees) by borrowers and lenders alike. The result is that the borrowers get better terms than would otherwise be available from ordinary bankers. The guarantee mitigates the risk—and bankers are in the business of risk.

The details aside, the beauty of the SBA program is that it helps small business owners pursue a dream. In this book, I want to show small business owners the benefits of owning their own property rather than leasing in much the same way that residential homeowners are benefitted when they own property.

Owning one's own home is the American dream, or so we've heard for years from Freddie Mac and Fannie Mae, the Federal Home Loan Mortgage Corp. and the Federal National Mortgage Association respectively, which have helped many to make that possible. Small business owners too can pursue a similar dream, one of growing business wealth, and securing a future through ownership of their commercial real estate.

How We Can Help

Most small businesses find it a lot easier to come up with 10 percent down than 20 or 35 percent down, which is just one way the 504 program is more affordable. It makes the dream possible, and that's what we're all about at Mercantile Capital Corporation.

Since this is all we do, we have become a key advocate for the small business owner, coordinating the plays. We act as quarterback. If a client hasn't yet met with a commercial real estate agent, we can put him or her in touch with one of proven competence. We walk clients through the entire process: how much they will need to put down, what interest rates they will see, how much to expect in monthly payments, and so forth.

For years, we've advised small businesses to get preapproved for a loan if they're contemplating purchasing a property. That's much the same as for first-time home buyers who know what they can afford by becoming preapproved. You don't want a real estate broker to waste your time by showing you $3 million commercial properties when you can only afford $300,000 ones. Some salespeople continue to confuse activity with results. If they have a four-hour window with you, they'll drive you around to see four or six properties, and if you like one, they'll suggest you make an offer. They don't consider that most commercial properties are not bought with cash, so it's essential to bring the financing aspects into play.

The Best-Kept Secret

There are a variety of reasons that commercial real estate can be right for you. In this book, I will help you with the specifics of pursuing the SBA 504 program to acquire such property as efficiently and inexpensively as possible. If you've heard of the program, you may have thought it wasn't right for you because of the many myths surrounding it.

Many readers, I'm sure, haven't even heard of this loan program. The great majority of my clients had never heard of it until they started using it, and that's why I call it the best-kept secret in the commercial real estate financing industry.

One reason you don't hear about the 504 program from lenders is that loan officers are typically compensated partly on the assets they bring to their banks or to their lending company. Those assets will partly depend on the kind of loans made and the loan sizes. An SBA 504 loan, as you will see later, is split between the lender and a government-guaranteed bond, which means fewer assets (amount of the loan) for the lender, and a smaller commission for the loan officer.

But, frankly, a chief reason that the 504 is not better known is that it's a government program, and though the government may have some very good programs, it isn't very good at marketing what it does. It has never been good at getting the word out about these programs. Instead, it relies on private sector lenders like me to deliver the news and educate the marketplace.

"Fulfilling Dreams Through Smarter Financing®"

Home ownership builds communities, as has been shown time and time again. The pride and responsibilities of ownership motivate active participation in civic affairs. It is human nature to take better care of what one owns. It is the antidote to apathy and blight. Neighborhoods where most people own their homes tend to flourish, and those stable neighborhoods become the building blocks for a more stable society.

Take that a step further, and you can see the parallels to owning your own business property. Small businesses constitute the backbone of our economy, and those that own commercial real estate and use it to plan for a more prosperous future are helping to produce a more stable economy, in many regards.

"Fulfilling Dreams Through Smarter Financing®" is the motto and vision for Mercantile Capital Corporation. We believe we are doing just that for small business owners nationwide. We help them take the next step. Many have already set themselves on the path to independence by becoming home owners, fulfilling the "traditional" American dream. By establishing a business, they have become their own boss, a goal that so many of us embrace.

What's next in this progression to personal freedom? Ownership of the facility in which that business operates, a home for your enterprise. It's the catalyst for making other dreams happen. By ceasing to throw money away on rent, you can build the kind of wealth that will bring you a care-free retirement when you can get off the treadmill and relax with the kind of freedoms you imagined would be yours. You will have the time, finally, to travel, to pursue outside interests and hobbies, to volunteer, and mentor.

This will likely be the largest purchase of your life and the biggest investment in creating wealth for your future. Done with foresight and care, your investment can set you on a course to generating wealth that will outlast you, that may buttress your family for generations. As you pay off your commercial mortgage, you will be growing assets to span lifetimes. You will be building a legacy. It's the next American dream.

Consider the story of Christine Finan, a native of Scotland, who moved to the United States about ten years ago and opened her own business called Aabsolute Massage and Skin Care.

Christine learned the key tenets of business from her grandfather, whose most valuable advice, she thought, was to make sure she owned not only her business but the building that housed it. "It may be a chicken coop," she recalls him saying, "but it's your chicken coop."

It wasn't long before Christine and her husband, Gerry, started looking into buying their building, scouting around for the best deal.

"After eliciting quotes from several different banks and lending institutions, we felt that MCC best suited what we were trying to accomplish with the monies we had to attain that goal," recalled Gerry. "Their loan program worked very well for us by allowing us to acquire the property with a reasonable down payment, which was not like the offers we received from some of the better-known lending institutions. We are very excited about it."

I tell people all the time that while we are technically in the commercial lending business, our primary goal is to make small business owners' dreams come true. We can relate to people like Christine and Gerry because we've been in their shoes. We've had to meet payroll every two weeks too, and we understand how important cash can be. We also know that to people like Christine and Gerry, buying their building is the largest purchase they've ever made.

To accomplish a dream, you will need to do things right. You will need the help of professionals and advisers: you want to structure every step intelligently. That's what we mean by the second half of our motto, "through smarter financing." It's important that you take a close look at your business plan and budget and put your capital to the best possible uses. That's how I hope to help you, the small business owner and entrepreneur, with this book.

But in introducing small business owners to the SmartChoice® Commercial Loan (as we like to call the SBA 504) as a prime wealth creation strategy, I also wish to reach out to those who play a role in helping them: the commercial real estate brokers and mortgage brokers, for example. They often are the ones to find the best deals on behalf of their buyers, who may lack the time and energy to do so by themselves. I also want to reach out to accounting firms and attorneys and financial planners who focus on small businesses, and I want to reach the many economic developers who do so much for communities and would appreciate knowing more about how certain government loan programs operate.

In short, this book, though it speaks directly to "you" as a small business owner, is also meant as a tool for those who advise small businesses.

This is the truth that I wish to impart: The SmartChoice® Commercial Loan, aka the SBA 504, is the way to go for longer-term financing that won't crimp cash flow, for lower interest rates that allow more of your payments to cover principal, and for smaller down payments. Short of getting 100 percent financing, which, like riding a rainbow or finding a unicorn, just isn't going to happen, it's the next best thing.

CHAPTER ONE

Why Own Rather than Rent?

Landlords grow rich in their sleep.
—JOHN STUART MILL

Things may come to those who wait... but only the things left by those who hustle.
—ABRAHAM LINCOLN

There's a story about Michael S. Dell, founder of Dell Computer Corp., that gets to the heart of why many business owners conclude they want to own their property rather than rent it. It's told by James Champy and Nitin Nohria in their book *The Arc of Ambition: Defining the Leadership Journey.*

Whether in business, science, or the arts, one must keep open to fresh ideas, the authors write. They asked Michael S. Dell, billionaire founder of Dell Computer Corp., whether as a boy he had dreamed of a future in technology. No, he replied, and began talking about flagpoles. It seems that when he was a child, being driven to school in Houston, he noticed so many buildings with stately flagpoles out front. He aspired to have some for himself someday. The authors asked Dell if he'd attained his goals. "Yes," he replied, "and I've got three flagpoles."

As ingenuous as Dell's childhood dream seemed, it was the foundation of fabulous success. His business savvy took him to great heights, but the ownership of commercial property, in and of itself, can indeed create great wealth. Even in the recent troubled times that the real estate market went through, the principle holds true: "Real estate cannot be lost or stolen, nor can it be carried away," said Franklin Delano Roosevelt. When purchased and managed with care, "it is about the safest investment in the world."

The value of home ownership has stood the test of time. Your salary pays the bills, but ultimately your fortune arises from what's behind that picket fence. Likewise, men and women of business also can grow their assets in more than one way. They are striving for success through entrepreneurship by being their own boss, but they can also build their wealth through the bricks and mortar of the building that houses their business, and the good earth beneath it.

We all sort of know it intuitively. You have to have a place to live. If you own a business, you have to have somewhere to run it. If you've gotten to a point where you have the financial means to pay a mortgage, you're going to ultimately own the place and build equity in it. Why would you just throw that money away? Why would you just give it to somebody else? Renting always has to be considered a temporary measure. It's common when starting out. It doesn't make sense long term. You can easily pay the same kind of money, if not less in some cases, to own that asset.

Among the many advantages of owning versus leasing, an important one is the ability to control your facility cost. You can do that with fixed rate financing when you buy your own property. You don't always have that option if you're renting the facility. A lot of times, an escalator clause in your lease will mean it's a variable cost to your business year after year, or every three years, or every five years, and that makes the budget planning more difficult.

You Have Arrived

There is another significant reason to own your commercial property, and this is more of an emotional reason, something that a lot of people can't articulate. It is similar to how people feel when moving from a leased apartment to a home they own. It's this idea that you've arrived, that you deserve it, that you've earned it, that it's about time you have your own little castle. You might recall that memorable scene in the movie *It's a Wonderful Life* when George Bailey helps Mr. Giuseppe Martini move into Bailey Park because George's savings-and-loan was financing his first home. It's a scene of joy.

Business owners too eventually often want a physical manifestation of their success. Some design their building from the ground up, including number of offices, layout, and signage, and watch as it rises. Tears of joy are not uncommon at our closings, even from the sternest-looking business owners.

That's a real factor that cannot be minimized. There are of course logical reasons for owning your own real estate, but there is an intense emotional reason also. It's natural and appropriate to feel that way. I understand the feeling. People don't often talk about that aspect of why they want to own their business property, and that's okay. Nothing's wrong with a little ego driving that action.

The Best Small Business Investment

Commercial real estate is an asset that can outlast the business itself. Once the enterprise has been sold, the businessperson can become the landlord. Ownership gives him or her a sense of freedom and self-direction, while continuing to build wealth.

It can indeed be the best investment a small business can make. Through the power of leveraging, significant equity is bound to build as the years pass, accompanied by the inherent tax advantages and income potential that commercial property ownership entails. Your monthly payments are making *you* rich, not the landlord. Those commercial mortgage payments may very well be less than you paid in rent, and they can be fixed, unlike those rents that inevitably rise from year to year. You have more control of your costs and your cash flow.

In short, you become the steward of the property where you conduct your business, and you can do with it as you wish. And as you enjoy that freedom, you are building toward another kind of freedom. You are creating a nest egg for a secure retirement and to share with your heirs. You are positioning yourself for freedom from financial constraints. A world of possibilities unfolds for pursuing your heart's desire.

And you can have as many flags as you ever imagined out in front of your building—*your* building. Just like Michael Dell.

Should You Continue Renting?

Despite the many advantages of owning commercial property, you may have good reason to postpone that dream for now and wait for the stars to align before you take that step.

Perhaps you have a great location. Maybe you're an attorney, a litigator who is renting an office right across the street from the courthouse, and it's highly convenient and advantageous. Or perhaps you just have no option to buy. You may be in a great location for your office, but the landlord knows it's a great location, and he's not about to sell it to you. There are definitely solid reasons for continuing to lease.

Uncertainty about your business cycles is also a consideration. Leasing gives you more flexibility than owning, of course, but every week people contact me about purchasing commercial property when they haven't even started a business yet, or it was just launched. They've read about us in some publication or on the Web. Often I will talk them down off the ledge. They're so eager to dive in, but when you're starting out, you have to use your precious capital wisely. The best thing you can do is to prove your business first. Prove your concept. Make sure that your products or services are established in the marketplace.

Then, and only then, does it makes sense to purchase property. That's usually after a few years, once you're confident you're going to be around for a while. By that time, you have a healthy customer base and profits. You have proved that you can compete. That's usually when the lightbulb moment comes. It's when you want to look at buying your own real estate.

If you do it before that, you could threaten the livelihood of your business, because you're going to take away capital that otherwise would have contributed to its growth, to help it survive and thrive. You're putting it into real estate which, at the end of the day, helps you, as the owner of your business, but doesn't necessarily do anything for the business itself. The business is still going to pay rent; it's just that the rent will be going to you, the owner, as opposed to the landlord. So you have to be careful, and make sure you get to that sustainable point before you contemplate buying.

Now, you may wonder whether the market conditions are just right for your purchase, but conditions never will be perfect, so how you define "right time" is somewhat difficult, especially in the wake of the Great Recession and panic. I often tell people that there is no perfect business deal right now. In fact, there may never have been a "perfect" business deal. If both parties in the transaction left a little bit on the table and are a little bit unhappy and feel they didn't quite get everything they wanted, that probably means it was a pretty fair deal. When one side comes out feeling way on top, something's probably wrong.

Consider Your Options Carefully

I once turned down a deal with a prospective client who was excited about buying a building and converting it into the shape of an ice cream cone. It would be the ultimate advertising sign, he said. No, I told him, that's not for me. Someday he would want to sell that building, I explained, and nobody would give a lick.

I counsel people frequently to be careful, when building or buying property, to consider the resale value. Don't build, for example, the Taj Mahal of day cares. It may be a great day care, certainly, and in a wonderful location, but day cares are a specific type of building, serving a specific purpose. Long-term, you may never get back out the value that you put into it. Obviously, you can enhance value by customizing a more multipurpose building such as an office building or industrial warehouse, but you must be careful. It's a fine line. You want to create your unique image, but you don't want to devalue the property by greatly limiting its uses.

Still, in some markets, people need to be a little more open-minded about how they might convert a building. For example, we've converted about a dozen and a half former restaurant facilities into nice office buildings. Now, a lot of people would look at such properties and presume that only another restaurant would be appropriate there. We helped our clients see that those properties, once you took out the kitchen equipment and added some demising walls, would make great office buildings, well located with plenty of parking. That's not something that a lot of people would necessarily think about on the surface.

As you consider your options, you also likely will be busy running your business, so be sure to give yourself plenty of time to make a good decision and handle the details. Your time is valuable, and you must use it wisely. You must not make such a large purchase on a whim, nor because your lease is expiring in a month or two and you need to *do* something. I strongly suggest allowing yourself six to twelve months. It can certainly happen a lot more quickly than that, but six months is sufficient to get fairly organized.

A Buyer's or a Seller's Market?

I think it's always good to consider whether the current market is thought to be a buyer's or a seller's. That, of course, will depend not only on the prevailing national economy and realty trends but also on local conditions. A qualified real estate broker will help you sort through what makes sense for you: what to buy, where, and the timing (I've provided a list of reputable firms in Appendix B to make this easier for you).

Clearly, the prevailing climate has been a buyer's market. Commercial property has been discounted everywhere you look. In fact, in some areas, it has recently been discounted as much as 65 percent to 70 percent from its high just a few short years ago. Also, we currently live in a historic low-interest-rate environment, and it doesn't have anywhere to go but up from here, though I do not expect to worry about increasing rates for a few more years. But even then, the fifty-year average rate on commercial real estate is about 8.5 percent. Recently we've been at about 60 percent of that average, so it has made a lot more sense to purchase these days.

In this market, with favorable valuations and rates, and with the tax advantages of ownership, business owners are finding it much more affordable to buy property than lease space. In other words, their mortgage payments are less than rental payments, and they're creating equity with an appreciable asset.

Identifying Your Needs

When deciding whether and when you're going to purchase a property, you have to do an assessment of your business needs. You will want, of course, to look for a facility appropriate for what you do or make or sell. A physician won't be looking at industrial warehouses, for instance. You can accomplish much with renovations, but that will add a lot to your expenses and you must factor those in and decide whether it would still make sense for you to proceed.

Consider the range of facilities and services that your company will need. Will your employees and your clients need plenty of parking? Do you anticipate you will need increasingly more office space? Do you need dock-high loading space for a warehouse? Do you want your property to be in a high-traffic area so it can be seen by potential customers?

For some businesses, being well-located is crucial—for example, the attorney who feels he needs to be close to the courthouse (or the jail)—but a lot of small businesses have more flexibility. They don't necessarily have to be in high-traffic areas. It really depends on how many customers come to visit you and how often. Many businesses operate primarily via telephone, fax, and e-mail with customers who often are located many states away (such as my firm). Customers don't necessarily come to the office very often, but if you have a retail or other business that depends on customers visiting you, those traffic and parking issues will be critical, as well as how much competition you will face in the community.

You will also want to find out whether the zoning allows you to use the property as you intend. This comes up a lot with clients who want to purchase old houses for use as, say, a day care, or for law or medical offices. If it's zoned for residential use, it cannot be used for a commercial purpose unless it has dual zoning, and it will not be eligible for commercial financing. You would have to pursue residential financing, and you would also have to deal with whether your municipality would grant you a variance to allow you to conduct your business there. You may find that municipal zoning restrictions prevent you from setting up a business in a specific area.

On the other hand, your municipality may offer economic development incentives to encourage you to set up a business in very specific neighborhoods. You can obtain significant tax breaks in such designated opportunity zones. There also are government incentive programs that can help small businesses through grants that might subsidize the down payments for property purchases. We recently closed a second 504 loan for a client in Maine who received a portion of his down payment capital from the state's economic development program.

You can review many such considerations with a competent real estate broker, but often the decisions are common sense. If you are currently leasing a facility, you likely already dealt with these considerations when you decided where to set up shop. You chose the area where you wanted to do businesses, the kind of property, the needs that it addressed, and unless those needs have radically changed, those same considerations will probably play into your decisions about purchasing a parcel of property, as well.

When you are seriously considering the purchase of a specific property, however, a professional inspection is in order. For one thing, you will want to know about any code violations or structural deficiencies that could greatly add to your costs. Such issues very well could lead you to abandon the prospect of that particular purchase, and if you determine that additional work and rehabbing are well worth the effort, those expenses often can be included in the financing. If you're going to do work that will enhance the value of your investment, it's a smart choice to include those costs in your loan rather than pay out of pocket for the work later. You likely will want to keep that capital available for other business uses.

In general, as you evaluate advantages and pitfalls of a particular property, your decision will come down to that oft-heard adage in real estate: it's all about location, location, location—how you will be using the property, how it compares with other such properties in your area, and its potential for resale.

Should You Buy Both Buildings and Land?

That is ideal. After all, no more land is being created, so it's better to own not just the building but the ground on which it sits. That adds value if you sell the property later. You have more control because you're not going to be restricted by your landlord, as happens in ground-lease situations.

It also eases the financing if you are purchasing both building and land. Lenders always will look at the worst-case scenario. They have to consider how they would dispose of your property in the event of foreclosure. If it happens to be a piece of property that's on leased land, the lender is responsible not just for real estate taxes, not just for insurance, but also for covering that monthly lease payment. Depending on the situation, that lease payment could be substantial. It's enough to drive away many lenders from all but fee-simple real estate deals (as opposed to lease-fee).

Some ground leases will be with a municipality or port authority or the like, and those often entail very small payments over many years, perhaps a century, because the land has been leased for economic development reasons. However, the payments likely will be much higher when the payments are with a private-sector developer. From the perspective of a lending company, those hefty payments would be an additional carrying cost while waiting to dispose of the property if you were to default on your loan.

Therefore if you *can* own the land, it makes a lot of sense to do so. Often it will give you room to grow, which is always an important consideration. I frequently advise prospective clients that it's a good idea to purchase a property with 25 percent to 30 percent excess of the needed square footage (or even some excess land). They may think they don't need it now, but they very well might need it later as their business grows.

I also often advise them that it would make sense to sublet some of that space. That doesn't work for every business, but for many it's common sense. If you can sublet some of the space you don't currently need, you can offset some of your mortgage payment. You need to be careful, however, if you're going to sublet some of your space and you're a fast growing company. If you think you're going to need that extra 2,000 square feet within a few years, perhaps you should limit any lease to a year.

One client of ours, a financial planner, was able to sublet about 35 percent of the space in his office condo that we financed. By doing so, he was able to cover his entire commercial mortgage payment just from the rental payments he received from his tenants. It made great sense for him, even though he was a relatively small operator who might never decide to expand and use the extra space himself.

To have someone else covering your mortgage payment is a tremendously advantageous situation. That's why I always advocate purchasing property where you have some expansion capabilities.

How Long Has the Property Been on the Market?

A good broker will be able to uncover how long a property has been on the market, and usually that's an indicator for your negotiations. If the property has been on the market for, say, fourteen months, you will have much more leverage in negotiations than you would if the property had come on the market just a month earlier. You might think the property is overpriced, but if it is a recent listing, the owner is far more likely to hunker down and try to get his price. If it's been on the market longer, the owner will think twice about dismissing you. You see that with residential sales all the time, and the same thing is going to take place on the commercial side. A good broker will know that and will try to use that to your advantage.

If it has been on the market that long, of course, you need to figure out why. Why hasn't it sold? Maybe it's a poorly laid-out building with all sorts of strange walls and small offices. Maybe it has one of those gigantic atriums that leaks when it rains and is tough to heat and cool. Aesthetic reasons that the seller thinks are fantastic features may be the very reasons the property hasn't sold. It could be overpriced. It could have a zoning problem. You never know, but the seller might know. The longer it's been on the market, the more you should suspect something is wrong or "different," and the more you can expect room for negotiation.

Assembling a Good Team to Help You

Smart small business owners and entrepreneurs understand they can't do it all themselves. They have to rely on others. The bigger you get, the faster you grow, the more it matters that you have a great team around you to help you accomplish your goals. You need the same type of competent team both for selecting commercial property and going through with the purchase. If you're a widget manufacturer (or yes, even a physician), it's kind of silly to think that you're going to be an expert at identifying commercial property, knowing exactly how to refurbish it, and knowing how to finance that purchase and those renovations. It's entirely unrealistic to think that.

So, it helps to surround yourself with people who have those talents as their specialization. Frankly, the better the team and the more it understands your needs and goals, the less you need to be involved in this process, and the more you can continue your focus on what you're good at doing: running your business.

A good leader should know how to delegate, but unfortunately a lot of small business owners are slow in refining that skill. By the time you're ready to buy property, hopefully you've learned those delegation skills and have realized how best to spend your time. And that is *not* driving around by yourself checking out industrial buildings all over town. Rather, it's to get preapproved for a loan with a commercial lender and call the best-known commercial real estate broker in your area to describe exactly what you're looking to buy, what you can afford, and how much you can finance.

The broker will then look for prospective properties, and neither your time nor the broker's is wasted. You may only see three properties out of the hundreds that might have been shown to you. Those will hopefully be the three that best fit your parameters in terms of square footage, location, type of facility, and so on. How many parking spaces do you need? Do you want a single-story or multi-story building? You'll have given a description of your ideal property to your broker, who will save you time by narrowing the range of possibilities.

If you try to micromanage and do it all yourself, you're likely to make mistakes because you lack the expertise. Mistakes can cost a lot of money. Some mistakes are inevitable. There's no perfect situation, and you could overlook a good deal, but you want to keep that possibility to an absolute minimum. The better your team, the less chance for errors. That's why you get a property inspector, for instance. You don't want to find out, two weeks after you closed on your property and a storm blows through, that the roof wasn't nearly as solid as you thought it was. Hiring a competent property inspector saves you heartache down the road. It's the same with the others on your team: the lender you choose, your real estate broker, and so on.

Good advice when making hard choices makes all the difference, and there are many who need that advice. There are about

26.5 million small businesses in the United States, of which about 7 million have employees.

The Lender's Risk vs. Your Risk

Traditional lenders have often gotten in the way of private enterprise in the pursuit of this dream of commercial ownership. Ordinary lenders are in the risk management game. When they look at a small business's financials, they are examining the past. Most of the time they do not look at projections the way a private equity firm or venture capital firm would. Therefore, if they're looking backward and trying to manage their risk, part of how they cover their risk is not to advance as much debt on property as perhaps you would like. They will want more in the form of capital up front: your down payment. That's one reason ordinary lenders require a much higher down payment than a SmartChoice® Commercial Loan requires. The lenders are offsetting their risk.

The problem for you, the small business owner, is that the more you put down on a piece of property, the less you have to deploy elsewhere, whether for growing your business or for a rainy-day fund. Ordinary lenders want a higher down payment to reduce their risk, but you as the business owner should strive to put down less, to reduce *your* risk. Small business owners need to be cognizant of this inherent conflict.

The SmartChoice® Commercial Loan that we offer is the best solution for the small business owner. Frankly, it's the best solution for the lenders too, because it minimizes their risk by having a portion of the transaction be a government-guaranteed bond. It makes so much more sense than requiring the small business owner to scrounge up

20 percent to 35 percent of the purchase price to put down as cash, as well as the closing cost and some of the renovations.

Capital used that way won't even produce revenue, in most cases. You might be able to rent out some of your space, and you can always exempt some of your mortgage payment from taxes by taking an expense for interest, depreciation, and amortization. But producing revenue isn't why you buy commercial property. You buy it because you're trying to create wealth long-term and avoid throwing money away on rent. In doing so, you want to stretch your dollar as best you can, and that's why I have long encouraged the SmartChoice® Commercial Loan and even have one myself.

By satisfying the needs of the lender, the SmartChoice® loan also makes the purchase of commercial real estate more affordable for a small business. Consider the recent market for commercial real estate: properties have been on sale at a deep discount; interest rates are at historical lows; and through a SmartChoice® loan you may only have to put down 10 percent of the total project amount. More small business owners can afford to buy now because of those three favorable variables.

The entrepreneurial spirit feeds the dream of owning commercial property. Unfortunately, traditional lenders sometimes make demands that are detrimental to private enterprises, and business owners often conclude that their goal of financing commercial real estate is unattainable. Nonetheless, there is hope and a wealth of opportunities, as we shall see.

CLIENT SPOTLIGHT

MAX CLARK, FINANCIAL BUILDING SERVICES
POMPANO BEACH, FL

Max Clark is president of Financial Building Services. FBS specializes in construction services for the financial services industry, including installation of ATMs and other bank equipment as well as inventory control and consulting.

How did you get started in this industry?

The business opened in 1989, and it came about as a result of a request from a very good customer of mine, Barnett Bank. They were getting ready to replace about 800 Docutel ATMs, and they had no single contractor to do that. At the time I was working for Diebold, Inc., as a sales representative. I happened to sit in on a meeting in which Barnett was discussing this issue of needing someone to do this for them, and I raised my hand and said, "I can do it." They said, "No, you work for Diebold, and we're buying NCR." "Yes, I can," I replied. So, they gave me fourteen sites. I quit Diebold and started the company in my bedroom.

My wife, Denise, was an account manager for ADP, so she was able to support us the first year. We hired some subcontractors, did the first fourteen machines, and they gave us 826 to do after that.

*What is the extent of the service you do on ATM machines?
Is it refurbishing or repairs?*

We are actually a bank equipment dealer for things such as bank vaults, drive-ups, and alarm and camera systems. As far as ATMs are concerned, we sell, refurbish, and "rig"— that is, install—them as a registered NCR dealer. We do not service them, but we do bring them live. We load all of the software and do all of the voice data cabling as well as the hookups. We do all of the construction related to it, so we are already a state-certified electrical contractor and state-certified general contractor.

How many locations do you have?

We have five offices: Pompano Beach, which is our corporate office; Jacksonville, Florida, which is our refurbishment center; Atlanta; Charlotte; and San Antonio. I had a very good customer who requested that we do some work for them in Texas, and we gladly obliged. They had such a large amount of work that they eventually asked if we would open an office out there. They had a rigging company that was going bankrupt and had stiffed them for several jobs. I basically bought out that company, hired their people, and took over their warehouses. We sent one of our managers out there, and it's gone fairly well so far.

How many employees do you have now?

We have forty-two full-time employees, and we use subcontractors in some places.

Why did you decide to start your own business?

At the time, Diebold had changed a lot. It had been a customer-oriented company since it started more than 125 years ago. The primary concern was always the customer. In the mid to late '80s, more and more emphasis was put on the bottom line, and the customer basically came in second or third. Nothing against Diebold. I still say it's the best company I've ever worked for. They had just grown into such a huge company, having merged with IBM (their ATM group). Things really changed, and I was a little dissatisfied with that. Denise and I talked about it a lot—that Diebold had gotten to the point where it was very difficult to work *with* them and *for* them—and I decided that it was time for me to go. When this opportunity arose, I knew ATMs and I knew rigging, and it just seemed like a good fit.

At the time, were there other companies doing this?

There were a lot of them, and there still are. In my industry, there are actually three large companies—four large companies, we being one of them, thank goodness! Then there are about 200 to 300 mom-and-pop [businesses], but the industry has evolved to the point that you have to be a registered rigger now in order to work for any of the major ATM suppliers. So we are registered obviously with NCR, Diebold, Triton, Wincor, with all of the major ATM manufacturers, which allows us to provide a complete line of services for banks relating to their ATM projects.

Do you see a trend in the industry going from those big multiton ATMs to the smaller ones?

No, not really. We typically only provide services to financial institutions, and we've seen a trend in the industry to maintain the same unit size but provide more services from the same unit. NCR is getting ready to roll out a machine that allows you to make any sort of deposit, including cashing a check through the ATM. Regions are going to be the beta test, and we'll start seeing more bells and whistles adding value to these machines.

How do you market your company?

Simply by word of mouth; we don't advertise. We do have a website, but the majority of our marketing is word of mouth.

We have extremely long-standing relationships. About 75 to 80 percent of our business is from repeat customers. Our major customers are all of the major banks, basically, in the Southeast. We don't work outside the Southeast and the Southwest. We just did our first install in Las Vegas, but the bank is based in Montgomery, Alabama. So, we pretty much stay in our area, unless we are requested to go somewhere else.

I mentioned the other "big three" companies; two of them are nationwide, but they only have project managers in each office. They don't have their own riggers. We are unique in that we have our own people in every office, our own riggers, and our own vehicles and equipment. It's easier, from a management standpoint, but much more expensive. The clients like it because they will have the same people doing the rigging for them every time. We make sure that our people are really well trained in customer relations. We typically try to hire tradesmen (carpenters, bricklayers, etc.) because they are obviously very good at what they do. Plus, most of them are really great people, a little rough around the edges sometimes, but you can work with that. We have been really successful with that method.

You effectively control everything for your clients.
Right. Many of these other companies sub out a lot of the work. We probably have the least amount of installation problems of any installation company in the business because we do the rigging ourselves.

Can you think of a reason no one else has picked up on this?
I think probably the cost. You incur more costs and have a lot more to worry about when you use your own people rather than subcontractors. That's why most general construction companies don't have their own people; they sub out the majority of the work, which is much less expensive.

But I'm sure that by delivering a much better experience for your customer you're able to price for that.
No, our prices are pretty much set. We are on national contracts with all of our big customers, and typically these contracts run from two to five years. Our pricing does rise

incrementally over time, but it really doesn't cover the cost; it's basically just a cost-of-living increase.

You have a very unique website, ATMsrus.com. How long ago did you come up with that?

Actually, when we started the company. We saw that everybody else used their company names as the website address, and we decided to do something a little different. Plus, I had just bought a toy for one of my grandkids from Toys "R" Us, and thought that it was a cool idea.

What do you have planned long term, since you are a fairly young guy?

Well, I actually want to retire. I have a really nice boat and was just told that I have to sell it because I don't use it enough!

So, no other major expansion plans?

No, I don't think so. We are expanding more into the bank security equipment segment, which I have done my whole career. We actually just got a major contract with a construction company to do all of the bank security equipment— the pneumatics, alarms, cameras, etc., for the new Indian River County government complex.

How much is your family involved in the business?

I have five children. I have a daughter who manages our Charlotte office, and her husband is the lead installer up there. He was a union electrician and decided that he liked this better, so she moved up with her children and took over that office and has been very successful. Our oldest son manages the Atlanta office, and two of our sons are the lead field people, one in Florida and one in Georgia. The youngest daughter is sort of doing her own thing.

I'd say it's the best thing we've ever done. If you ask my children, they'll tell you that they work harder than anyone else here. They get nothing for free. When we hand out the bonuses, they get exactly what everyone else gets. They are our children, but they are also a part of this company. We make a huge effort to not show partiality to anyone here. We want everyone to feel that they're a significant part of the company. Just because you are a Clark doesn't mean you get any special treatment. If anything, we are harder on them than anyone else. They will all be very successful one of these days.

MCC financed two of your properties. Why did you decide to stop renting and start owning?
I think just the fact that I'm old-fashioned and that I really like to see something that I'm paying for. I don't lease a single vehicle. I have twenty-six trucks, and I don't lease a single one of them, and no one can believe it. It probably makes better business sense to lease the vehicles, but I'm just old-fashioned.

Denise and I ran some numbers one day, and we just about had a heart attack over how much rent we were paying. We're now thinking about buying a building in Charlotte, since that office has been open for two years now and is doing very well.

We didn't want to do that in the beginning. We wanted to see how things played out. Also, we are probably going to buy a building in Atlanta since that office is showing profits that normally take longer to show. Right now, I don't have any plans to buy a building in Texas. I want to wait and see how that works out.

A major reason to buy the properties is so that Denise will have a good income when the "old man" is no longer here, if I go first. That's really the thought process: to make sure that she and the kids are taken care of. You know, this building has probably appreciated 15 percent since we bought it two years ago.

The Jacksonville office is holding steady, and one of these days that will start to grow. The other two areas, Atlanta and Charlotte, are booming right now. I mean they are absolutely booming. Two of the three largest banks in the country are based in Charlotte, and they have no intention of leaving. So, it's just one of the most vibrant cities you will ever see. It's just amazing what's happening out there for us.

What was it that brought you to us? Why did you choose us?
Honestly, your personality, to begin with. When we called you the first time, you were very upbeat and positive. I believe you were excited about just starting your business,

but you haven't changed. We had several options, but the fact that you were very attentive was very important to me. You know once it happens, I become extremely loyal—so you know, but I think that the personality of the company really won me over.

Our regular customers, or what we call business-as-usual customers, pay a premium for us. They know that, and they're willing to do it because of the service they get. They also know that if they don't get the service that they want, all they have to do is pick up the phone. My favorite expression is, "It's never a problem; it's a situation." If we don't take care of it, then it's a problem, but we don't have problems here; we have situations. One of my greatest points of pride is that we have never ever missed an installation date. Thirty thousand and never missed an installation date. Now we've had instances where a customer decided not to do it, but as far as concerns what we're responsible for, we have never missed an installation date, and that, to me, is invaluable. It's just an amazing feat, and we work very hard at doing it. The more we grow, obviously, the harder it will be to maintain this sort of track record, but it was a real point of pride for me for years and still is.

The other thing I'm very proud of is that we have never lost an existing customer. The only way we lose customers is through acquisitions and mergers, and then we tend to gain the surviving entity in those situations, so I'm fairly proud of that as well.

What is your fondest memory in your business career up to this point?

I think just seeing the employees being *fairly* happy, though no employee is ever *really* happy. Also, two years ago, four of our employees received their ten-year presents. Four have been here for at least ten years; three have been here more than fifteen years, and one of them has been with us since the day we started. We decided to honor these people with a getaway to Daytona, and we took our entire company. We brought everybody and their families and their children and honored these four that have gotten their Ten Year. Two of them are sons, but we did ask the other two, and their answers really made us feel good. They said it's because we are their family. We really want to make it that way for every one of our employees.

What is the biggest lesson you have learned in your working experience?

I've learned so many. I think it's that you can't trust everyone. I hate to say that in an interview, but I think that is the biggest lesson that I have learned. I was sort of naïve coming into this business. I thought that everybody we worked hard for and did a good job for would continue to allow us to work for them, or at least give us the opportunity, but that's not the case. Several of our employees have even gone out on their own and are now competition. Competition is fine; I don't mind that. I just would have preferred that they told me up front, but of course that is their prerogative. I guess I could say that the biggest lesson is to better assess people and businesses.

When I get a new employee or a new account, I try to really delve into what kind of an account it's going to be, what kind of employee he or she is going to be. You have to make sure that you take care of that account and take care of your employees, who are basically on the same plane. One is no more important than the other. If you don't have the good employees, then you don't have the good accounts.

How do you make your company stand out from the others that you are bidding against?
I think it has to do with our service, and it's twofold. One is the fact that we can provide the service in-house, ourselves. The other is that we are capable of doing complete turnkey services for the banks. We provide the architectural work, the engineering, the construction, the electronic voicing data, the equipment, and the loading of the software. We can take it from concept to actually putting the cash in the machine, and hand it to the customer. We let them do their banking and we take care of the whole thing. When it's time for the ATM to open, we're ready.

To what would you attribute your biggest success up to this point?
I think being honest and forthright. I think those two, and perseverance. I live by perseverance. If you read the plaque on my wall, you will see that you don't have to be the best educated, the prettiest, the biggest. As long as you persevere, the chances are really good that you are going to succeed. For a high-school dropout, I think I've done fairly well. I came back and finished high school, but I wanted

to be a warrior and went to Vietnam. I wanted to go fight. Since I was fighting in school all of the time, I figured it was better to go and fight somewhere else!

What kind of advice would you give to other small businesses?

If they are dealing with customers—to be honest with those customers; to provide good service; to be prudent with their company (and by that I mean don't take everything from the company, but give something back); and to recognize their employees and what their employees actually do for the company. Without them, there is no company. Make sure they understand how important they are.

I think that's just about it: be honest; provide good service; and maybe, above all, recognize your employees. Listen to them (sometimes they are a hell of a lot smarter than me) because they are out there all of the time. You can't have an ego if you want to succeed as a small business.

CHAPTER TWO

Getting Organized

As a rule, we find what we look for; we achieve what we get ready for.
—JAMES CASH PENNEY

*While the worriers are worrying, the planners are planning and the accountants
are figuring out why we can't afford it, I'm busy getting it started.*
—WALT DISNEY

Time means money. Every one of us, unless somebody has created a time machine, only has twenty-four hours in a day and seven days in a week. As a successful businessperson, you must use your precious hours wisely, and that means understanding what your hours are worth and organizing your days and your life so as not to squander your most valuable asset: time.

When I was a kid, I spent plenty of time mowing yards and raking leaves, running my own business. I don't do that today not only because I'd prefer not to be out in the blazing Florida heat, but also because it's probably not the best use of my time. It's not a very high-value thing for me to be doing, especially when I can hire the neighborhood kid to do it. He does a pretty good job, by the way, and it teaches him something about entrepreneurship and further develops his work ethic.

In other words, you have to always contemplate what else you could be doing. I like editing. Chances are I have edited anything that my company puts out and that communicates to the outside world. I feel I have a knack for the words and figuring out how to communicate our message. I spend a fair amount of time on that because it comes to me naturally, and I can see its fundamental importance to our growth.

However, there are things I don't do: I don't underwrite credits anymore. I know *how* to underwrite credits, but it's no longer for me. If we get much busier, I'm going to have to start underwriting credits, but that's not a really high-value use of my time. Again, it's that old concept of opportunity cost. What else could you be doing with your time and money that would bring more value to you? What opportunities do you forgo, and how much do you lose, by focusing on less worthy pursuits?

A high-value use of my time is to get more clients in the door. I use my time well when I can expose our ideas to a broader base of people and educate the marketplace better about how to utilize the type of financing that we do. It benefits our company when I can help small business owners so that they don't have to put so much money down on a piece of property, slowing down their business growth, because they didn't know any better. I'm the one who communicates best the importance of long-term wealth creation through the purchase of commercial property.

Most people understand that they have only so much time and money, and they have to use it as wisely as possible, and that's all the more reason to work with specialists. You don't want to be somebody else's guinea pig.

It helps to know what your time is worth. Take how much you made last year and divide by how many hours you worked, and the result is what an hour of your working time is worth. You should know that figure, and if you want to make more money in the next year, do the same calculation based on a higher amount that you want to earn. That way, anytime you find yourself doing some silly little task, understand the opportunity cost to you. You'll never get that hour back. Understanding that is enlightening and motivating.

I find that thinking about the value of my time keeps me on task. I'm ruthless about not wasting it, and I think that's been a big part of my success over the years in the many things I do. Every hour, every day counts. That's how dreams happen: one day at a time, but you can't plan for a future, you can't even dream unless you first can settle some of the details that will advance that dream. If you don't, your dream could turn out to be delusional. You have to get that grip on reality.

If you assess what you want years down the road in your retirement, owning commercial property can truly be a huge step toward realizing those goals. Your space becomes a moneymaking venture for you rather than the money-losing venture that it is when you pay rent. If you can convert your rental payments into a commercial mortgage payment, and you've saved a little bit of money to get your down payment to buy the property and to get a SmartChoice® Commercial Loan, especially in a time of favorable interest rates and good deals to be found on properties for sale, you might very well be able to buy more cheaply than you can rent, and when you do, you will effectively be paying *yourself* rent, rather than paying it to some landlord so he can cover his own mortgage.

In time, you're going to own a significant chunk of a valuable asset. Ultimately, if you hold it long enough, it could be debt-free, and perhaps you will be able to lease out some of the space and become a landlord yourself. The monthly rental check is a joy—when *you* are the landlord.

It comes down to a simple strategy of converting your rental payment into your mortgage payment. It's going from leasing to owning. It makes all the difference in the world. You can create wealth for yourself, whether or not you have grand visions about the future. It's a step toward the financial freedom that you will need later in life, once you've long since decided to stop operating your business.

Getting Your Act Together

Toward that end, I cannot overemphasize the importance of good organization in effectively pursuing the purchase of commercial property. Your alternative is confusion, and sometimes chaos, not to mention probable denials on your commercial loan application.

If you don't get organized before you apply for your commercial loan, you are setting up a barrier for yourself. Anyone who borrows money, even a Donald Trump, will feel some level of anxiety until the lender signs off on that commitment letter. The better organized you are, the more likely you will get a fair look from your lender.

You must manage your time and not waste it. Let's say you want to buy some commercial property, and you have noticed a commercial real estate broker's signs all over town. You think he must be the guy to call, even though you don't know whether he has the right specialty or even does sales, not just leases. Does he represent tenants primarily, or does he mostly handle purchases and sales? Does he specialize only in a certain part of town, without much knowledge of other parts? You can't know until you investigate.

Let's say that you find a real estate broker you intend to work with. You're looking for a 10,000-square-foot office warehouse in a particular part of town, and you're available Thursday afternoon. He picks you up at your office and takes you for a drive to that part of town to start looking at 10,000-square-foot office warehouses. Some of them cost $600,000, and others are a couple of million dollars. That's a pretty broad range, and there could be all sorts of reasons for it, but which can you afford? You don't really know. You haven't bothered to determine whether you can afford just the $600,000 building or perhaps the $2 million one. Or maybe you should be looking at a $300,000 building, or none at all, for now? Instead of looking for 10,000 square feet now, maybe you really should be looking at 12,000 or 14,000 square feet to give yourself some room for expansion and/or to sublet some of the space?

So many considerations, but it all starts with getting yourself organized, knowing the documentation that the commercial lender is going to need, and ideally saying to the lender that you select: "Take a look at this and tell me how financeable I am. How much could I borrow if I needed to? I understand that for anything below that financeable amount, the chances are good that you'll approve me, but tell me what's the upper limit?" In having this discussion, you won't waste your time shopping for buildings you cannot purchase.

Preapproval: A Critical Step

You were probably preapproved before you went shopping for a house. You also should be preapproved with a commercial lender before shopping for a "home" for your business. Because your time is so valuable and you cannot afford to waste it, you need to make sure you know what you can afford and what you are able to finance before you go out with a commercial real estate broker looking at properties. Often, commercial real estate brokers don't urge their potential clients to get preapproval. They just want to go out and show them properties. That doesn't make a lot of sense. A preapproval gives you the advantage of moving quickly once the right property comes up for sale, which, depending on the market, might not be often.

People often overlook this critical step. Instead, they will fall in love with a particular property, and they'll then try to figure out some way to get it financed. The same thing happens in the residential world. A young couple falls in love with a particular house, and they end up depleting their entire savings so they can get in there. They probably had no business looking at that house to begin with, but the real estate agent showed them the house because it was on the map and on the route. The agent's commission depends on the sale price of the property, as is the case in the commercial property world, so he or she has an incentive to show you properties that are much more expensive than you might be able to afford.

So, you need to be careful with this, and the best thing to do is to know what you can afford before you go shopping. Some shoppers are concerned that obtaining preapproval will show their cards and tip off the seller on how much they have available to spend. However, you generally won't be showing your financial information to the broker. You attach your terms, your financial statements, to the information you provide to your commercial lender. All bankers are held to a very high standard of privacy and confidentiality. It's a red flag to me if somebody wants to borrow money, but then they don't want to show us their tax returns. It's going to be really hard to borrow money from us, or any other legitimate lender, without disclosing those to us.

You must share your financial information so your lender can compute your financing range, but that doesn't mean you need to disclose to your commercial real estate broker how financeable you are. You can keep that to yourself if you're concerned the broker will try to push you toward the higher end of your "approved" spectrum. Instead, tell your broker your needs. Say, you're in 10,000 square feet now, want to have some room to grow, so maybe you can look at up to 15,000-square-foot facilities. Describe the amenities you need, and the parking requirements, and how many offices you ideally would like to set up. Let the broker know the part of town you prefer and then see if he can find a facility within the spectrum of what you can finance for your business.

Documents You Will Need

For a loan preapproval (which not every lender does, by the way), you will need seven basic documents: three personal ones, four corporate ones.

If you've settled on a particular property and you're planning significant renovations, it's helpful to know what those renovations might be, so we can factor those into the project amount. For a preapproval, of course, you won't likely know just what those renovations might entail, but the other seven documents here will help your lender determine how much you can finance.

Here are the seven documents you will need:

- Three years of **personal tax returns** and three years of **corporate tax returns**. If your business has not been around three years, you would provide your lender with as many tax returns as you have. If it's just one year, however, consider that your financing will likely be more problematic, and it may be premature for you to be purchasing real estate. Also, if you have less than three years of business tax returns, the SBA will likely want to see a business plan from you with at least two years of detailed assumptions.

- A **personal financial statement** and **business financial statements** (with an income statement [P&L] and a balance sheet). It usually is best to have figures that are fairly current, within sixty to ninety days, so that your lender can see how your business has been performing lately. For your business, you'll also need to submit an **interim financial statement for the previous year** that covers the same time period as the current financial statement.

- An **authorization to release your personal credit information**. This tells your lender what kinds of debt you're obligated to repay. A lender like us will need that to calculate whether you are likely to be able to maintain your lifestyle if you proceed with the property purchase, as well as consider the credit score the bureaus have given you.

- **Schedule of business liabilities**. This tells your lender what kind of

Checklist for Pre-Approval

The following is a list of documents required by Mercantile Capital Corporation in order to issue a firm Pre-Approval Letter. This process is completed in 24 hours or less, and gives each small business owner an accurate picture of what he or she can expect when talking to commercial lenders. The complete package (with forms included) can be found at www.504Experts.com.

Personal Documents
- Authorization to Release Information/PATRIOT Act Compliance.
- SBA Personal Financial Statement (Form 413).
- Previous three years of complete personal tax returns (required for all proprietors, partners, and stockholders owning 20% or more of voting stock, and all guarantors).

(continued...)

business debts that you have, because they'll have to factor that into the equation as well.

When we analyze all these numbers from the documents above, we're basically looking for the cash available from your operating business to service (pay for) this new debt for the commercial property. We also have to contemplate whether there are any existing corporate debts, such as big equipment leases or lines of credit that you are paying. We have to consider what kind of personal obligations you have. You don't want to be in a situation where you're straining to cover your personal obligations just to buy this piece of property.

Down the road, we'll need other documents—investment records, bank statements—to get some verification that you actually have the capital to put down as your equity injection for the down payment, but we don't necessarily need that upfront, certainly not for a preapproval letter. If the total project amount is a million dollars, requiring $100,000

Operating Business Documents

- Business Schedule of Liabilities.
- Previous three years of operating company tax returns, and accountant-prepared or company-prepared year-end Balance Sheets and Income Statements (P&L) for the previous three years. If a change in ownership occurred, you'll need to provide the seller's financial statement for the past three years.
- Current Interim Financial Statement of operating business —Balance Sheet and Income Statement (P&L)—dated less than 60 days old.
- Previous year Interim Financial Statement of operating business as of the same date as Current Interim Financial Statement, for year-over-year comparison. (For example, if Current Interim Financial Statement is dated 4/30/12, you'll need to provide an interim statement dated 4/30/11.)

Property Documents

- A breakdown of the costs associated with the project will need to be submitted as well, if known. (For instance, a commercial real estate contract, an estimate of renovation costs, etc.)

down, and you tell us you have that much in a business or personal account, we will accept that. As we get closer to the closing table, we'll need to get it verified.

If the buyer lacks the organization to produce this kind of documentation, then he probably shouldn't undertake the project. We do need potential borrowers to have a basic level of sophistication so that we can analyze their documents and make sure they're financeable.

At the end of the day, what every lender is trying to determine is this: Will this person pay me back or not? If you're a bit of a mess—you don't even know where you put your tax returns from two years ago; you don't have financial statements since this time last year; and you have no idea quite what you are worth on your personal financial statement and can't recall what your business debts are—chances are you have no business buying commercial property.

What Lenders Are Evaluating: The Five Cs

The five Cs of lending are a time-tested way of understanding how you are being evaluated when you apply for a loan. They are collateral, cash flow, credit, character, and conditions.

- **Collateral:** The lender—and you—will want to make sure that the property you're buying is worth what you're paying for it. The lender doesn't want to advance you a $1 million dollar loan on a property that's only worth $500,000 dollars (although that's hardly a likely scenario, since in almost every case you're going to be required to get a current commercial property appraisal). The property you're purchasing is the lender's collateral, so it must have the potential to cover the loan if for some reason you don't. If a piece of property is particularly old, you may not be able to get a twenty-five-year or even a thirty-year amortization on it for commercial financing. You may only get a fifteen-year or a twenty-year amortization, because the thinking is that it may need to be replaced or substantially renovated sooner than twenty-five years. Also, lenders often will only lend money on equipment with terms of five, seven, or ten years, because a lot of equipment doesn't have a useful life beyond ten years, and so that's something they will consider as well.

- **Cash flow:** This is sometimes also called "capacity." The lender is looking to see how much cash the business generates along with examining the amount of existing and proposed debt. It's a simple formula. We're looking at the net income of your operating business. If you're going from leasing to owning, the lender will be considering such figures as your current rental payments, plus noncash expenses such as depreciation, amortization, and interest costs. The resulting figure is the total cash available to service the proposed debt on the proposed property. That amount might be changed, up or down, once the lender examines your personal debt obligations. If the owner's income is more than enough to cover personal obligations, we call that a situation with "owner excess" and the cash-available figure can rise. Otherwise, we may have what's called an "owner's draw," which will lessen the cash-available figure. Once we derive a figure for cash available to service the debt, we compare it to the amount of the annual debt payments, and that gives us a ratio. A lender might say, for example, that cash flow is "1 to 1," or that the DSCR (debt service coverage ratio) is 1.4 times or 1.2 times coverage.

In most cases, at an absolute minimum, you want to have at least a dollar of cash available (annually) to cover every dollar of annual debt service payments. Ideally, however, to assure yourself that you're going to get financed, oftentimes you will need $1.25 to cover every dollar of that annual payment. In the case of a hospitality loan, a lot of times, most lenders have upped the ante even further and maybe it's $1.40 for every dollar of debt service payments. So in that case the lender would say it's a 1.4 times coverage.

The lender will also evaluate whether you will have sufficient capital to successfully run your business once you've made the down payment and budgeted your debt service payments. It would be pointless for you to take out a loan that choked your enterprise so much from a cash flow perspective.

- **Credit analysis** tells us about your history of making good on your debts and other obligations. You want to have your credit scores as high as possible, though the rankings and their fluctuations can be a mystery. The scores are a range from 400 to 850. If your score is in the 800s, that's considered phenomenal. The average in America right now is about 680. We don't generally like to lend to people who have less than about a 650 credit score. Most of our borrowers are in the 700s, but sometimes we do lend to people with a score of less than 650, if they have a reasonable explanation. Maybe they're disputing some medical claims against them or perhaps something has been reported incorrectly by the credit bureau. There are a number of possible explanations, and we'll certainly consider all appropriate ones.

Often, multiple owners of a small business are making a purchase, so we're not looking at just one borrower's credit scores we're looking at all the guarantors' scores. Let's say you have three people who each own a third of a business. Two of them have credit scores of 750 and one has a 580, but the latter is going through a divorce and the spouse decided to run up all the credit cards and didn't make any payments for several months in a row. This is where commercial lending becomes a bit of an art and not just science. For some lenders, that 580 score will be a deal killer. Others, like us, will certainly take the explanation into account.

- **Character** is another factor that a lender will consider carefully, and one indication comes from the credit score itself. Numerous late payments suggest that you don't manage your debts responsibly. Some of these considerations can be very subjective: do people know you, and what is your reputation? Using the credit score is one way to keep this analysis a bit more objective. The lender will want to know, for example, if there has been a bankruptcy and how recently.

- **Conditions** of your industry and the economy also play a role in whether you will get a commercial loan. The lender wants to analyze how things have been shaping up for your kind of business in your region. No one thing is necessarily going to knock you out of the running for a loan approval, but lenders do include such evaluations to help them decide whether you would be a good borrower to take on. Again, it ultimately comes down to their quite understandable concern that things could go south; would they get their money back from you? I list conditions last because oftentimes these are out of a borrower's control. Unfortunately for many small business owners lately, many banks have made conditions one of their major criteria in underwriting due to the lackluster economic recovery we've experienced.

CLIENT SPOTLIGHT

ROBERT FRADY, THE MELTING POT
LONGWOOD, FLORIDA

Robert Frady is the co-owner and franchisee of The Melting Pot, a fondue restaurant that specializes in unique, interactive dining experiences. After Robert and his business partner achieved success with their first location in Raleigh, North Carolina, they moved to Central Florida to take ownership of a new location in Longwood. Mercantile Capital Corporation helped finance the acquisition of their Longwood location, as well as the addition of an outdoor patio seating area which increased the capacity of the restaurant by 20 percent.

How did you get started with the Melting Pot and this industry?

When I was in college in Tallahassee back in 1980, it was one of only three Melting Pots at that time, and I got a job working in the kitchen there. Eventually, I moved out to serving, and I stayed there my entire college career. It obviously paid my way through school. I was there from '80 through the first part of '85, and while I was there, the gentleman who owned that restaurant had this crazy idea that he would buy the concept from the originators in Maitland, Florida. He did it in '83, I believe, and he decided to franchise the concept out.

My partner, Dale, started working there about a year after me, also in the kitchen at first, and then as a server. We were both hotel/restaurant majors, and we thought, "What the heck?" We worked there for three or four years, and we saw how people responded to it. We thought it was a concept that "had legs." So we talked to the folks we were working with and expressed an interest in buying a franchise, and we were one of their first franchisees in 1985. Straight out of college into owning a restaurant. We moved to Raleigh, North Carolina, and spent about eight or nine months just trying to find a location and someone to lend us money. Nobody would lend to us, of course. We're two guys, fresh out of college, with a crazy idea for a fondue restaurant! One thing led to another, and we had a couple of family members loan us a little money and cosign on a loan for us. We opened the first store up there in '85, and we've been doing it ever since.

Long story short, we eventually moved back to Florida, and the Maitland location came up for sale in 1990. Like they say: You can take the boys out of Florida, but you can't take Florida out of the boys. We were looking for an opportunity to move back to Florida, and when that restaurant came up for sale, we bought it right away and have owned it ever since. We eventually sold our restaurant in Raleigh later in '91, and that's where we stand today.

Was there a store in Gainesville?

There's still a store in Gainesville. We actually own the property there. We bought it in '98 from the lady who owned it. She had owned it since its inception around '83, I think, so, the Melting Pot had been there about fifteen years already. She had some health issues and needed to get out. So we bought the location, but it was a chore for us to operate, being an hour and a half away. We'd have to travel and stay overnight in Gainesville. It just wasn't an ideal situation. When we decided to purchase the restaurant, the opportunity to own the real estate was what was really appealing to us. So we sold the restaurant (the business), but we held on to the real estate, and we leased that out to the new owner of that Melting Pot.

That's awfully smart.

It worked out okay. It just gave us an opportunity to get a little bit of real estate and then not have to operate the business. Day in and day out, the restaurant business is nickel and dime. I mean, you really need operators in there watching your money, your cash flow, and things like that. With us being here in the Maitland area, it just made more sense for us to be property owners in Gainesville.

What made you and Dale want to go into business for yourselves?

Well, I think we just saw an opportunity. We were in on the ground floor. Now, there are 105 Melting Pots. We were the second franchise for the people who bought the concept in '83. The first restaurant opened in Kendall [North Carolina] about two months before we opened in Raleigh, so it was almost simultaneous. Basically, we were right there in the beginning, and we just saw an opportunity. Again, we had worked in a Melting Pot, waiting tables five nights a week for three or four years. I had a chance to see how people responded to it. It was new; it was different. It's not a restaurant in the sense that you had to have culinary skills to run it. It's more like a business, little bit of a "glorified deli," if you will. I would say that it runs more like a business than a restaurant, if that makes sense. We were business majors and restaurant majors, and we believed it was something that was going to work. We might have been young and naïve—maybe we got lucky—but we succeeded, and we're still doing it. Hopefully we'll do it until we retire. If we can get another fifteen or twenty years out of it, we'll be fine.

Tell me a little bit about the concept.
We like to say we "specialize in creating memories." It's a unique place for folks to dine. It's not like Chinese or Italian [restaurants]. People are not going to do it every week or even twice a week, but what we find is loyalty with our guests, people that will come back year after year. The Maitland store just celebrated its thirtieth anniversary last year, and we now see people who ate at the Melting Pot with their parents bringing their kids in. So, we build a good loyal base of customers.

Again, it's not a high-frequency dining experience, but it's something that people think about when that special occasion comes up, that birthday, that anniversary, when they have relatives in town. That's kind of what we specialize in. From a service standpoint, I think there's a lot of guest interaction, so our service staff is very important. We have to hire the right people, train them properly, and let them sell the experience to people.

The food is excellent. We serve the highest quality foods that we can find, from the cheese fondue through to the chocolate dessert, but I don't think the food is what sells the Melting Pot. I think it's the experience that sells the Melting Pot. We have to manage that experience and make sure that it is at its best in all aspects from the facilities to the service. It's a little bit unique, I think, in that way.

Who do you consider your main competition with this unique concept?

We're a little bit of a niche. One thing that guests are concerned with is that we're at a high price point. We're above your chain restaurants, if you will. We're above Outback and Carrabba's, and those places which are more mainstream. We're probably closer to a Fleming's or a Roy's from a price point, and maybe an experience standpoint. Some of the market pricing is really in line with Ruth's Chris, a really upscale restaurant, but we're not fine dining. We're fun dining. There's a difference. We're kind of our own. From a price standpoint I'd say we're upper steakhouse almost, not casual dining by any means. We're not casual, but we're not fine dining either. We kind of have our own little niche, I think, in that way.

How do you market your company? Is it mostly word of mouth, through the experience?

Yeah. That's what works in the restaurant business, to be honest with you. We do mass marketing, some neighborhood marketing certainly. A little bit of discount marketing through entertainment publications, that type of thing.

We're trying to reach new guests, but you go to the restaurant business by word of mouth more than anything, I think. It's what they call four walls marketing. Inside these four walls, that's where most of your marketing is done every night. There's an old saying that the easiest thing to do in the restaurant business is to get someone to come in and try it. The hardest thing to do is get them to come back again and again and again and again.

What made you want to own the property rather than lease it?
Well, you know, honestly, for us it was almost a no-brainer because the numbers just worked out. I mean, we were looking at somewhere in the neighborhood with rent and taxes around $7,000 a month, and then to purchase we were going to be in the high eights to $9,000 a month. So it just made more sense. We have the property in Gainesville and the opportunity to own this property, for our retirement down the road.

Dale and I are in our forties. He's forty-six, and I'm forty-five. Even at this age it comes up quickly. Fifteen to twenty years—we've got a twenty-year mortgage here—puts me right at retirement time, and then we can make decisions, and we will have some real estate. So we really just thought it was a good investment. We certainly paid a market price that may be a little bit higher, but that's what the owner wanted, and looking down the road, it still made sense for us to own the property.

There were a couple of other things there, too. There are some road projects and things that are going to be happening here. We felt it was to our benefit to be in an ownership position rather than a leasing position with those things happening. Plus, it gave us an income that we could use to improve the property. We added the outdoor seating, which allowed us to get a full liquor bar, and all those things are going to make it a much better restaurant.

Why did you choose MCC to do the financing?
Actually you were recommended by our realtor. We had talked to two other lenders at the time, and then we met with Mercantile, and we just compared the deals, and you were the best.

What is your fondest memory in your business career?
I would say opening this location, for me, because it was a big step. We had been located right down the street for ten years, behind the Albertson's shopping center there, toiling away, making ends meet, but not really making any money. We were doing a volume of about $800,000 to $850,000 a year, and we just believed in our heart that we had established this area of clientele here, and that this location was going to make such a huge difference for us with the exposure, and it has.

The first year we were up about 50 percent. We're probably up about 40 percent in annual sales over that location, and that's a big deal. We thought it would be; we were excited about building out the restaurant. We did a lot of the work here ourselves in terms of project management. We did a lot of hammering and nailing too, but it was just an exciting thing for us to do, I think. There have been a lot of them, but I'd say opening this restaurant was probably our biggest moment—so far anyway.

What is the biggest obstacle you've faced?

Generally it's labor, although I would say that for us the last few years it hasn't been as much. I would say in the last couple of years it's been cost, obviously. Fuel has affected us like everybody because we're getting fuel charges on all of our deliveries now, and then you have the storms. Last year I had a 25 percent increase on my premiums for insurance. This year it went up another 30 percent. So I think right now inflation factors in a little bit. It's kind of hidden in the costs. They don't talk about it, but if you run a business, you know it's there.

What's next?

We're looking to next year opening another location in the Waterford Lakes (Oviedo, Florida) area. We've actually already negotiated and have a lease to sign for that any day now, and when we get that store opened, we're going to close our Maitland store.

It just makes more sense from an economic standpoint. We're not going to fight for the same customers all the time. At Maitland we did a million dollars last year, which is a first, but we struggled to get there, and cash flow takes care of everything in business. If you could move up to million two or million three, that's a huge difference from a cash flow perspective. So we're about that. And we're certain that the Waterford location will do that.

But what is that going to do to my volume here and to Maitland? So from a sensible standpoint, it just makes sense to let that store go; spread out our locations. I'd rather have two restaurants doing a million and a half than three restaurants doing a million.

What would you say is the biggest lesson that you've learned throughout owning, working?
I think I've learned how to manage people better. When we opened our first restaurant in Raleigh, North Carolina, I was twenty-five or twenty-six years old. So what did I know about running a business and managing people? And there were a lot of pressures there, and we were just barely surviving, for the most part.

I think I've learned how to fine-tune my management style over time, kind of lead by example and by showing. You can't just tell them what you want. You have to show them that you're an integral part of that too, and then they buy into it. If it's important to me, and I demonstrate that by the way I interact with the guests every night, then when I tell you it's important for you, you understand that's what we need to be successful.

So I think just learning how to manage people over the years, and maybe leading by example a little bit, and knowing when you have to turn the screws a little bit and when not to. It's been huge to actually let go of some authority and delegate things to your managers, and let them take care of things, and trust that they'll do the same job.

To what would you attribute your success?
I think Dale and my partnership is a big part of it. Dale and I are lifelong friends. We grew up together. I'm talking childhood friends. We went to high school together. He was always a year ahead of me. He graduated, went away for a little bit. At some point we wound up back at Florida State, roommates together. Then working together at the Melting Pot, and then we came up with this idea that we're going to open this business together, and everybody said, "You don't open a business with your best friend. You guys are going to hate each other. You're going to ruin everything."

But for Dale and I, it's worked. We respect each other immensely. I trust him. We've been on the same page with anything that was important from the beginning, whether it was buying this property or opening this location, doing the location in Sand Lake, buying Gainesville when we did, and buying the real estate.

A lot of families and friendships have been split up by trying to go into business together, and we've just been very lucky that never happened to us.

Do you have any advice for other small business owners?

I would say just follow your instincts, and stay true to what you believe in. It doesn't mean you don't listen to people and learn from folks who might be wiser than you in certain areas, but if you have a real belief in a small business that you think is going to work or a concept that you think can work, then I would say to follow your heart.

How was your experience working with us through the process?

Oh, it was great, yeah. I understand there's always going to be timing issues when you're dealing with the federal government. We knew that when we went into the process. And actually I think the program is great for folks exactly like Dale and me. It allowed us to stretch our capital. Putting 10 percent down as opposed to 20 or 25 percent is huge. Maybe there's no possible way for you to come up with 20 or 25 percent. So you're using your experience, your credit, and the little bit of money you have for leverage because that's really to me what it's all about. The more real estate or the more things that you own, the more leverage you create for yourself as you go down the line.

So I think it was a great program from that standpoint. It's ideal, again, for guys like us. We would have had to come up with literally twice the amount of capital that we did to make it happen. We were a little hesitant only because, when we initially went to borrow money to build this location, we spent literally a year with a local [lender] trying to do an SBA loan, and just had paperwork on top of paperwork.

We had finally, literally, signed the lease and we were ready to get started here, and we just told them to forget it. So we knew SBA lending. The guy who bought the restaurant from us in Gainesville used SBA, and he had the same experience. It took him literally a year and a half to get the lending through.

Now what you've convinced us is that you guys specialize in this; you can expedite those things. With you guys, we didn't have to worry about it. We gave you the information, and MCC took care of all the paperwork, and that's pretty much the way it went, so we were happy with it.

If that opportunity arises again, we'll certainly be knocking on your door again, that's for sure.

CHAPTER THREE

Finding a Good Real Estate Broker

The best way to predict the future is to create it.
—PETER DRUCKER

If you are not willing to risk the usual, you will have to settle for the ordinary.
—JIM ROHN

Whether you call him or her your agent or your broker, the person who works with you to locate a suitable commercial property to purchase for your business will play an important role in forging your future, so you must choose wisely. The word "agent," however, often connotes someone who works in residential real estate, and that's not really the person you need.

You don't want to go to the same person you dealt with when buying your house, even if that person is your brother-in-law or third cousin or whoever. More than likely, residential sales are all that person does. Your friend Sally probably has no idea about the nuances involved in commercial property deals, and she probably won't be offended if you pass her by, just as your family doctor wouldn't be offended if, under the circumstances, you opted to see a heart surgeon. Even if Sally is quite experienced, she might only do one commercial deal a year. You don't want to be her guinea pig.

You want to go to a specialist, generally known as a broker, who deals exclusively with commercial real estate. A specialist will be familiar with what needs to be done to expedite your purchase and will also know other specialists who will be helpful to you—a commercial property inspector, for example, who understands issues that a homeowner might never imagine. If you need to make renovations, you can probably tap your broker's network to find a competent general contractor, architect, and engineer who specialize in commercial properties as opposed to residential properties. There's a world of difference between commercial and residential when it comes to finding, purchasing, financing, renovating, and maintaining, and you need a team that knows what to do. You want to get to know the *right* people who know other *right* people. It opens doors to many of the *right* opportunities.

What you are looking for in a broker is someone to find those properties that meet your criteria. You may have decided on a particular square-footage need, a particular property-type need, a particular part of town, various access considerations, and a host of other specifics. You give the commercial real estate broker all these variables that matter to you, and the broker earns a commission by finding a property that meets as many of those variables as possible.

Let me emphasize the words "as possible." Sometimes you'll get really lucky and come across the perfect building and the perfect fit, but prepare yourself for the likelihood that if you are looking for ten attributes, you will get only eight or nine of them and will need to do renovations to attain the others. The property, or your plans, might need some adjusting.

Brokers are paid well for their services. Their commission, in general, is about 3 percent of the purchase price. The buy-side representative is making about 3 percent, and a lot of times, the sell-side rep is making about 3 percent. The bigger the project, the lower that percentage may be in some cases. Sometimes they're splitting 4 percent or 5 percent.

Qualities in a Good Broker

To find a good commercial real estate broker, it's always helpful for a small business owner to consult with his or her network. Talk to other small business owners who have bought properties. Whom did they use? Whom would they recommend? Even if they wouldn't recommend the broker, they may have worked with a contractor who pleased them. If you have a network like that, you're probably going to be able to get various names and contacts.

As in many things, you're looking for people of good character and integrity who will carry your flag and seek exactly what you want. You have probably had the experience of telling a residential real estate agent that you want a specific kind of house that cannot cost more than x dollars, just to be shown various houses that dramatically exceed that figure. You don't want to deal with somebody like that. You might consider a property that exceeds your budget by 10 percent, but if it's by 50 percent, you can reasonably conclude that the broker is just not listening.

Find out as much as you can about the broker. Ask for references or testimonials. Can you talk to some people the broker has worked with in the past? One indicator of a broker's success could be plenty of signs, billboards, or notices in the paper. That helps you to verify whether the broker is legitimate, though of course it's not failsafe.

It's a good idea to do an online search on anyone you're considering as a broker. Even if you've heard from two or three of your friends or associates that this is the best commercial real estate broker in this section of town for the property type you want, do a quick online search and see what comes up. You can expect to find information about the broker, and you very well may find comments from past clients or colleagues.

When you go to the broker's office, is it professionally appointed, or is it some guy in a garage? That's not to put down garages. Maybe it's a nice garage that's been converted into an office space, and maybe he specializes in auto repair shops. Who knows? Oftentimes a small operator can give you more personal service, but you can tell a lot from the vibes you get when you pay a visit to the person who will be helping you chart your future.

If you've heard good things about this person, if you've talked to him or her, if it's a fairly reputable firm, if you know other people who work for the firm, you will feel reassured. It's essential, though, that you get along on a personal level. People buy from people, and you have to enjoy working with them. If a guy is a phenomenal negotiator, you still might not be able to tolerate him if he's a real jerk. You might prefer someone of *acceptable* skills who is a truly decent person you enjoy. Personalities matter, and only you can decide what's right for you.

Commercial real estate brokers often specialize—for example, a retail specialist, or an industrial or office specialist—and these people don't necessarily mix, meaning you don't go to a retail guy to find properties that are industrial in nature, and you don't go to an industrial guy to find an office building. They each have their own silos, and that's where you go for what you need because they will have the right connections and referrals, they'll have a deeper understanding of what is and is not a good buy for you, who does the best repair work for that particular type of property, and other important concerns.

A big consideration is this: Does the broker know the market well? Commercial real estate brokers have a tendency to specialize not just by property type, but also by region. I know a broker here in the Orlando area who only likes to work in Seminole County, where I live. If you were a small business owner in Osceola County, he wouldn't want to go down there. It's too far away for him. He doesn't know the market there. He doesn't know the roads. He doesn't know the access points. He'd feel like a fish out of water. If you were looking for property on a rail spur for a big manufacturing plant, he could certainly find it eventually, but it would mean extra work on his part, and probably time and potential mistakes on your part. He just doesn't know that county as well as he knows Seminole County. In looking for a broker, you need to consider such geographic expertise.

Brokers should, of course, be accessible. You want to be able to reach them within a reasonable timeframe. I don't mean the broker should be on call 24/7, as some residential agents are. I think that's a little ridiculous. You wonder whether someone who offers that kind of service is valuing his time as much as he should. Unfortunately, that's what the marketplace expects from someone in the residential world of real estate. When dealing with a commercial real estate broker, I think it's reasonable, if you send an e-mail, text, or a phone message, to expect a response within a couple of hours, certainly that same day. The broker may or may not have an office full of high-tech equipment, but the principles of finding property are the same as they were a century ago.

When a truly professional broker realizes that you need someone else's expertise, he or she should refer you to a colleague who might be able to serve you better, but you won't know for sure whether that's going to happen, so do a bit of research on your own. You don't want to end up with someone who desperately needs a sale. Generalists sometimes push for a sale if they can find anything remotely close to what fits the bill, whether it serves your best interests or not. A deal like that could easily fall apart, wasting hours of your time. Working with specialists can spare you that frustration.

Often, specialists will know about properties that are about to come on the market that currently aren't listed anywhere, and that's valuable insight. They may be able to impart information to you that is not common knowledge and could be quite useful.

Sometimes it's the bigger commercial real estate brokerage firms, the well-known ones with established success that can serve you well. If you are working with somebody who has a CCIM designation (Certified Commercial Investment Member) or an SIOR designation (Society of Industrial and Office Realtors), you will have some assurance that he or she will provide a level of knowledge that you might not get otherwise. These designations mean the broker has spent considerable time to become more educated in commercial real estate. That can be very valuable for you.

Consider the names of the firms at which the broker works. Our company has a national relationship with CBRE, Lee & Associates, and Newmark Grubb Knight Frank (formerly Grubb & Ellis), some of the largest commercial real estate brokerage firms in the world. I used to be the chief financial officer at the NAI affiliate here in Orlando, NAI Realvest Partners, and NAI is also one of the world's largest. Cushman & Wakefield and Colliers and numerous others are reputable firms as well (I've provided a list of these national firms in Appendix B , and you'll only have to investigate to see if they have a presence in your town).

Remember, however, that regardless of which firm you choose, you are still dealing with individuals within it, so you still need to check out their reputations and get along personally with your broker. In general, these large, national firms should have some of the "higher-class" folks that are out there in the world of commercial real estate. You will be better off working with them than with firms, even the large ones that specialize in residential sales. If you're buying a house, those other firms are great, but you're not buying a house.

Your broker will be involved in the steps leading up to the sale. The broker should start by meeting with you to discuss what you're looking for, and then he should find out what's available and show it to you. You need to get out there and view the properties, kick the tires, so to speak, so you can get a good feel about what would work for your business. Once you decide, the broker can draft the contract with whoever is representing the seller.

Those are the functions for which your broker is paid. Many will be very helpful and friendly from a customer service standpoint. If you decide on a property that doesn't match your needs 100 percent—and that's quite likely in any market—your broker should be able to recommend quality contractors to help with renovations.

Hopefully, the broker will be looking out for your interests. Properties rarely sell for the listed price, and that's where negotiations come in. You can expect that a good commercial broker will negotiate for the best price possible. You'll put in an offer that's less than the list price and come to terms at a figure that's tolerable to the seller. If there are conditions at the property that need to be considered, those can be discussed during the negotiations and taken into consideration before finalizing a sales contract.

True professionals will want you to get the best deal even if it means their commission is lowered a bit when you negotiate less than list price. The broker knows that serving you well will enhance the chances that you will return in the future, as your business grows, to buy more property, or that you will refer the broker to your business friends.

Theoretically, you could go out and find your own property and negotiate with the seller yourself, but I don't advise it. You don't have the time, and you don't have the expertise. Those are the two biggest reasons. It's like going to trial and trying to represent yourself instead of hiring an attorney. In the words of Abraham Lincoln: "A man who represents himself has a fool for a client."

Questions to Ask Your Broker

Are you a full-time commercial real estate broker?

Some brokers work full time, while others use real estate as a second job for extra income. You don't typically see too many part-time brokers on the commercial side, as opposed to the residential side, but it's still worth asking. A full-time broker is more likely to specialize in the kind of property you want, while a part-time broker may be more of a generalist in real estate services. In addition, a full-time broker is easier to contact when you have questions.

Naturally, you will want to find someone who takes a serious approach to his profession. Look for someone who has dedicated a great deal of time researching and knowing the real estate market and can convey that knowledge to you easily.

How well do you know the area?

If you are considering a property in a different city or state, make sure the broker you are considering is familiar with the area. It would not be a good idea to work with someone who is not well acquainted with the area in which you are considering purchasing property. A broker's knowledge of the market will prove to be a valuable asset in your purchase process.

This is pretty important if you want to be in a particular part of town, for example, or close to your home. That is a "side benefit" that a lot of small business owners get by buying their own commercial property, by the way. If they're not so location dependent, meaning that they have to be in a certain part of town, then a lot of times most of them will try to be closer to their home to cut down on their commute time, and the closer you are to your home, the better *you* probably know the area too.

How much experience do you have in the industry?

It is important to find a broker who has worked in a particular market for a reasonable amount of time. If you are the broker's first client, you should find

Questions to Ask Real Estate Brokers

The following questions should be used to determine whether a particular commercial real estate broker is right for your project. Purchasing commercial property is one of the biggest decisions any small business owner will ever make, and you should feel comfortable with the professionals you work with at all stages of the process.

- Are you a full-time commercial real estate broker?
- How well do you know the area?
- How much experience do you have in the industry?
- What is your process for finding the right property?
- How long should the process take?
- How much time can you dedicate to my project and me?
- Can you refer me to a good commercial lender?
- Can I see other properties you have brokered?

If you don't get satisfactory answers to the above questions (and others you come up with on your own), don't hesitate to thank them for their time and move on to another commercial real estate broker.

someone with more experience. Let the beginners cut their teeth on someone else. That being said, I wouldn't get overly hung up on this because it would be better to have an expert in your property type and region than someone who has more years of experience. You could have a commercial real estate broker who is two or three years out of college, for instance, but already has a CCIM or SIOR designation, specializes in just what you need, and is aggressive. That could be ideal for you.

What is your process of finding property?

There are various online services such as LoopNet, CoStar, and Real Estate Directory News or Property Sourcebook that help brokers find out what's available. That's the first thing they're going to look into, and they'll hopefully know the area so well they can flip through their mental Rolodex. Brokers should block out some time to go out and take a look at what they've uncovered because a property's current condition may not match that pretty picture online.

How long should the process take?

It is a good idea to know in advance how long it will take to find a property and complete the entire purchase process. If your broker says it will take one month, be wary. Finding the right property and closing on it within one month is rare in the world of commercial real estate. You should anticipate the entire process will take about three months, assuming you find a property in a reasonable amount of time. Keep in mind that purchasing a commercial property involves many steps. Things are not as simple or automated as they are on the residential side.

This also *does* depend on your requirements. If you need a very specialized building, it will be more difficult to find. If you're just looking for a basic 10,000-square-foot office building and you can be anywhere within a ten-mile radius, it's going to be a lot easier than if you need a 50,000-square-foot manufacturing plant on the east side of town, close to a highway, and preferably with a rail spur. This is all a bit of a balancing act. You want to be as specific as you can, but hopefully your needs aren't so extremely specialized that it becomes difficult to find property. That's really what's going to affect how much time is involved. I've seen people decide on a property within a week of meeting with a broker. Others take years.

How much time can you dedicate to my project and me?

Be sure to ask this question during your initial interview. You want to know up front how accessible your broker will be. You do not want to learn the answer to this the hard way and fail to get updates and information when you need them. Your broker should be checking in with you regularly to tell you about new properties or update you on the status of your offer. You should not have to hunt your broker down. Test your broker: After your initial interview, call to see if he or she is responsive and gets back to you and how long it takes.

You want the broker to be busy. It's an indicator of success, but, if returning your calls takes two days or more, it might be smarter to work with someone else.

Can you refer me to a good commercial lender?

Once you've selected your property, the very next consideration is how you are going to pay for it. So many questions: Am I getting a fair price? What's going to be my down payment? What's going to be my monthly payment? Am I getting a fair interest rate? You should expect your broker to be able to direct you to the best people to answer those questions. After all, commercial real estate brokers don't get paid until your deal closes. They could dramatically expedite their income simply by providing referrals for you to commercial lenders and encouraging you to get preapproval. Again, time means money, and the sooner you get your financing, the sooner the broker has a commission in his pocket.

However, a lot of commercial real estate brokers, for whatever reason, don't seem to be wired to think about the financing. Well over 90 percent of commercial real estate is financed. You would think virtually every broker would have several commercial lenders to call upon, ones whom they respect, trust, and have used before for client referrals, but oddly, a lot don't do that. They're much more likely to know a couple of good general contractors to help do renovations, or a property inspector. Of course, if you've read this far, a call to us should be on your to-do list regardless.

Can I see other properties you have brokered?

It is a good idea to visit a few properties in your category of interest. This will give you a good idea of what your broker can find for you. Ask for references and a list of former clients. Call the referrals and find out if they were satisfied with the broker's services. This is a big decision for you. Don't hesitate to ask a broker's past clients about their experience—and really *do* call them. Studies show that references for job candidates rarely get called. *These* references should be because this may very well be the biggest purchase you ever make.

Also, if the broker doesn't have pictures of past deals on his wall or website, you'd be wise to ask about them. You're looking for verification that the broker is who he says he is and does what he says he will do. If you need an office building and all the photos on the wall are of warehouses, something isn't congruent there. If you need industrial space and you're driving around an industrial park with a broker who doesn't mention a single property there that he has handled, you might have an issue.

Let the Broker Do His Job

"If you want something done right, do it yourself." We have all heard that, and a lot of small-business people may live by that adage, but when it comes to commercial property purchases, you need to fight that urge. Chances are you don't know much about commercial real estate, and you need to rely on an expert. I've financed a lot of ophthalmologists. If I had something very wrong with my eyes, I'd go to an ophthalmologist. I wouldn't try a home remedy. The same thing applies for you. If you let a commercial real estate broker do his job, he or she can save you valuable time by zeroing in on the most likely prospects that will serve your needs and help you build wealth for a prosperous future.

CLIENT SPOTLIGHT

ROB MARLER AND BRIAN BANGLE, DIRECT WIRELESS
SANFORD, FLORIDA

Headquartered in Sanford, Florida, Direct Wireless was started by the partners, Rob Marler and Brian Bangle, to fill a gap in the cell phone accessories market. Marler and Bangle have seen their company grow tremendously and continue to be successful. MCC has had the pleasure of working with these entrepreneurs to finance three of their company's buildings

How did you get started in this industry?
Rob: When I first got out of college, I got started in the [cell phone] industry in 1993 up in Maryland. Brian and I started working for Nextel in 1997 and quickly became aware of a shortage in accessories and started this business after four months of being at Nextel.

Why did you decide to start your own business?
Rob: Well, I think freedom and being able to be the controllers of our own destiny.

Brian: I would agree with that—freedom, for sure. It's given us the ability to make decisions and do things to move in the direction that Rob and I see fit for our company.

As far as concerns the services that you offer—accessories, repairs, activations, etc.—you're a one-stop shop.

Rob: Yeah, absolutely, especially from the Nextel side. Now, with the Sprint merger, we are working our way toward being a one-stop shop for Sprint as well.

How did the merger affect you?

Rob: Positively. It opens us up to a much larger customer base and gives us service and repair opportunities for the twenty-plus million Sprint subscribers that came over. So, it should be good.

How many locations do you have other than this one?

Rob: We have seventeen in total, in five states in the Southeast.

Who do you consider to be your main competition?

Rob: Ourselves.

Brian: Yeah, I would say ourselves, absolutely.

Are you somewhat alone in what you do?

Rob: No, there are plenty of other people that do it. We're impacted by Sprint retail, big-box retail, and there are other companies like ours as well, but there is plenty of business out there for all of us. Brian and I have never worried about the competition. If we do what we need to do and do it well, everything will work out fine.

What do you do differently for your customers?

Brian: Well, I think we focus on the customer more than your average retail store. That would be what's different about what we do. We put a huge emphasis on the customer.

I'm sure that makes a big difference. How do you market your company in the industry?

Rob: Mainly through word of mouth and repeat business from our existing customers. In the past, Sprint and Nextel have given us co-op advertising dollars to use. We've spent tens of thousands of those dollars, and none of it has really been very effective. I think taking care of the customers to keep them coming back is the key, and then they'll tell their friends.

On the real estate side, what made you want to own your property rather than lease?

Rob: Well, there are a couple of things. We had been through two different headquarters-type buildings and outgrew them very rapidly, and we didn't want that to happen again. In both situations, we ended up on two different floors on different sides of the building. It was just crazy, and we wanted to try to avoid that. We also figured that, if we're going to get something we can grow with, we might as well look into getting into something that we could own instead of just paying rent. So, it just made sense.

How many locations do you own?

Rob: We own the two buildings here, and we own another building that is our repair facility—so, a total of three buildings. The other locations are smaller shops and are all leased. This location is our headquarters, and we ship product in and out of here. We also have all of our administrative capabilities here, so this is where we need the most facility and do the majority of our internal growth.

Why did you choose MCC to finance your commercial real estate?

Rob: I think originally it was through a relationship that MCC had with NAI because Mike Heidrich was our commercial real estate rep. We did shop conventional lenders, and most of them couldn't touch what you guys offered in terms of both down payment and rate at that particular time.

How would you describe your experience working with MCC?

Rob: Very good. Everyone was very attentive. We didn't have to wait for anything, so it was a very pleasant experience, and we've done it with you three times now.

We definitely spoke the same language. You're entrepreneurs and small business owners too. I have a lot of respect for both you and Geof. Geof is a long-time entrepreneur. He's been doing stuff for a long, long time and he's well respected in the community. You guys are good people for sure.

Brian: You're both extremely knowledgeable and motivated, so I think we've gained a lot from the relationship, and we probably still can moving forward. Anything we do, you'll probably be the first ones we call.

Rob: Yeah, we'll definitely be doing business with you guys again, without a doubt.

What's your fondest memory in your business career?
Brian: The fondest memories for me are the employees growing within the organization. When you can give a good raise or see an employee grow within the company, those are the best times for me.

Rob: When someone cries when you give them a raise or a promotion, that really is very rewarding, not necessarily the tears, but just their joy.

What's the biggest obstacle that you have faced in business?
Rob: People. When you have good ones, it's great, but it's hard to find the good ones. You know, we could definitely conquer the world if we had enough good people; it's just finding those good people.

Brian: That's really the challenge. A lot of people look at outside factors as obstacles, but we never do because we are willing to adapt and change to whatever the industry's needs and customers' needs are. Any real, true obstacles would be internal, such as employee challenges.

How do you two function together in the business? Do you handle different aspects or team up on a lot of things?

Brian: Well, a little of both. We do a lot of different things, though. Rob, as the president of the organization, handles a lot of communication with Nextel and Sprint and is currently handling a lot of the stores outside the state [of Florida]. I do a lot of stuff here internally and collaborate with Rob on other issues such as growing the business.

What's the biggest lesson you have learned in your work experience?

Rob: I think patience. It might not be a huge lesson, but patience is something that we've developed over time. In the past, our reaction to things was swift and aggressive, for good or for bad. Now I think we tend to sit back, look at things a little harder, and look at ramifications a little more than we have in the past. We don't get ourselves in as many difficult situations as we have in the past.

Is that also because of your size and that you now have people that depend on you?

Brian: I think—in terms of risk tolerance—we've found that you have to examine everything: the opportunities and the negatives and positives for making the leaps or the jumps from one level to the next.

Rob: When you get bigger, if you do make a mistake, the pain can be greater. Before, when we would grow, someone would say, "Do you want to open a location here?" We'd say, "Yes," and we'd just go do it without giving it a second thought. Fortunately, it's worked out; we've been able to muscle our way through every good and bad decision.

To what do you attribute your biggest success?

Rob: I think Brian and I are successful because we enjoy owning our business. I think too many times, entrepreneurs are in business just to make money, and I think those people who are in business just to make money are not as successful. I think our biggest success is owning the business for the right reasons: because we enjoy it and because we enjoy the people we work with, and we enjoy those moments when people are achieving and growing within our organization.

Do you have any advice for small business owners or entrepreneurs starting out on their own?

Rob: I think finding a mentor is important. You know, there is a lot of good information you can read in books, but finding a mentor who can help you is invaluable. Brian and I have had a few people over the years who have helped us. They really can help you avoid making a lot of really bad decisions. We've not made any really *bad* decisions. We've made some decisions that have cost us some money, but we've had some people along the way who have supported us and guided us down the right path. So, I think finding someone that knows something about business to support a new business would be a good thing.

Brian: I think that's a really good point. We didn't even consider having a mentor until probably a year and a half or two years into it, which we found to be very important.

I also think it's important to have a strong business plan as a road map. You have to know what the end result should look like, whether it's short-term or long-term, but then be able to deviate from that plan and be flexible. You have to be able to change and adapt as things come up, but I think it's definitely important to have a plan in place.

When you started, did you have the end in mind, or did you just set out to see what would happen?

Rob: Well, we've talked to several folks in private equity as well as venture capital-type people, and we just don't have an exit strategy right now. We really enjoy what we do. If someone came along and gave us a bunch of money, I'd be bored out of my mind. Brian and I are the kind of guys who, on Sunday night at seven o'clock, are looking forward to going to work on Monday morning. That's just the way we've always been, and we continue to be that way.

Brian: That's why I say it's good to have short-term and long-term goals, because you can actually see the achievement with short-term goals. I think with Rob and I, it's just constant achievement. I mean, what do you do when you meet your long-term goal, or get to the end of your exit strategy? I don't know what we would do. I'm not sure I can really think that far ahead. You just have to think, "How big do you want to get?" and, "How far do you want to go?"

Rob: I think above and beyond that, the question is, "How much fun do you want to have?" and, "How much do you want to enjoy what you do?" There's a tremendous amount of pain involved with growth. One of the real problems that I have with growth is that if you put a plan in place for growth, you almost bind yourself to making that happen. Some of those decisions, although they may be good today, may not be good in six months. It's tough to start putting infrastructure in place and start making decisions to do something and go somewhere when it might not be the best thing.

Brian: Six months is such a short time too, but in our world, it's a lifetime.

CHAPTER FOUR

Finding a Good Lender

I've learned ... that opportunities are never lost;
someone will take the ones you miss.
—ANDY ROONEY

Destiny is not a matter of chance, it is a matter of choice;
it is not a thing to be waited for; it is a thing to be achieved.
— WILLIAM JENNINGS BRYAN

L et's say you want to finance a commercial property that you're buying for a million dollars. You go first to the bank where you have all your accounts, which is a natural inclination since you're familiar with the people there.

"I'd like to buy that office building over at 10th and Main," you say.

"That's great," the banker says with a smile. "We'll need you to put 25 percent down."

Most conventional loans for commercial real estate, in the recent economic environment, have been 65 percent to 80 percent loan-to-value. You'll have to put up the remainder—20 percent to 35 percent—as a down payment. That's the current standard in the market for commercial real estate.

The conventional loan scenario is the easiest one for the banker. You'd get a loan for $650,000 to $800,000 on your million-dollar purchase. Bankers, like many people, often do what's easiest for them, and it can cause them more work when they involve an entity such as the SBA.

When you hear the figures, though, you scratch your head. "Gosh, that's a lot," you say. "I'm going to have to use a lot of my savings. I remember when I bought my first house, I only had to put down 5 percent. Don't you have something like that, something with a lower down payment for a small business guy like me?"

"Well, we *do* have something," the banker might say, if he or she has any expertise in the matter. "It's a small business loan program, and it may be perfect for you. What do you think of 10 percent down, maybe 20 percent? That should help you a little bit. How does that sound?"

"Great!" you say. You envision a down payment much easier to handle than the first figure you heard. You've now been introduced to the world of SBA loans.

Invariably, however, the SBA program that the banker will be talking about is the SBA 7(a) loan program. You often won't hear about the SBA 504 loan program, and the reason may be in the way the loans are structured.

From the banker's perspective, an SBA 7(a) loan would amount to $800,000 or $900,000 after the down payment is made. Lending the money conventionally, with the higher down payment, would mean only $650,000 to $800,000 for the banker, but in either case, the loan is structured so that it's in a first lien position (mortgage/trust deed).

You also could finance your commercial property purchase via an SBA 504 loan, which also often can be for only 10 percent

SBA 504 LOAN STRUCTURE

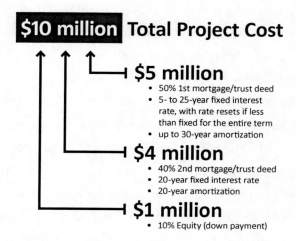

$10 million Total Project Cost

$5 million
- 50% 1st mortgage/trust deed
- 5- to 25-year fixed interest rate, with rate resets if less than fixed for the entire term
- up to 30-year amortization

$4 million
- 40% 2nd mortgage/trust deed
- 20-year fixed interest rate
- 20-year amortization

$1 million
- 10% Equity (down payment)

down, for a loan amount of $900,000 or more, since you can roll in closing costs and other "soft" costs. However, the loan is structured so that only 50 percent of the total cost, or $500,000, goes in the first mortgage/trust deed. Forty percent, or $400,000, is in a second mortgage/trust deed, and it is ultimately a government-guaranteed bond. The remaining 10 percent is your down payment.

Sample project cost of $1,000,000

Here's how an ordinary banker might look at three loan options for a typical commercial real estate purchase.

	Type of Loan	Loan Amount	For the Lender
Scenario A	Conventional	$650K – $800K	better
Scenario B	SBA 7(a)	$800K – $900K	best
Scenario C	SBA 504	$500K	good

Line those three options up on paper, the way a banker might look at them: Scenario A, a conventional loan for $650,000 to $800,000; Scenario B, an SBA 7(a) loan for $800,000 to $900,000; and Scenario C, an SBA 504 loan for just $500,000 (because that's the bank's portion that it ultimately will be lending and probably keeping in its portfolio).

This really becomes a pocketbook issue for the bank's loan officer, who is out in the trenches day in and day out and is partly compensated by the size of the loan (asset) he brings to the bank. He isn't being compensated on that $400,000 bond portion of a 504 loan, in most cases, and the 504 loan involves dealing with another entity, a Certified Development Company (or CDC), which is basically the SBA's eyes and ears for that second mortgage/trust deed (I've listed numerous CDCs and their contact information in Appendix A).

There are a number of informational videos on the Mercantile Capital Corporation YouTube Channel (youtube.com/504LoanExperts). You'll even find an entire playlist called "Education about the SBA 504 Loan" (among other things).

Therein lies what I've often referred to as the "dirty little secret" of why SBA 504 loans are not better known. We at Mercantile have made a major impact in spreading the word, but a lot of work remains to be done in educating the marketplace about the best loan product for an owner-occupied commercial real estate purchase. In fact, it's the primary reason you're reading this book, but I'll explain much more later.

What You Need in a Lender

Here's the first thing you want to find out about a lender: "Are you lending?" As silly as that may sound, in this day and age there are plenty of lenders that aren't. Commercial banks, particularly, have been under a tremendous amount of regulatory pressure to reduce their exposure to commercial real estate. In such a climate, it's not uncommon for banks to want to finance only the truly A+ credits and make it very difficult for anybody that might be even an A- or B+ credit.

Whether the lender has a national reach may or may not be helpful to you. The bigger question is whether they lend in your area. Again, if you're dealing with credit unions or banks, a lot of those lenders are restricted to certain geographic areas. Other than the "big boys," the household-name banks, very few have a national footprint, and the same applies to credit unions.

There are several basic questions that a small business owner must ask commercial lenders, and these questions should come early and yield clear answers so you can narrow your choices. For example, how much of a down payment will you need? That's the very first question I think every small business owner needs to ask a potential lender. Running a business entails strategic utilization of capital, and first and foremost, that means having the capital to utilize. Therefore, look for a lender who will accept the smallest down payment possible. This gives you and your business more flexibility, which means more options. Said differently: Keep your powder dry so it's available when you need it.

Another key consideration will be the length of the loan's amortization. The length will determine, to a large extent, how much you pay per month. Again, because of the recent regulatory environment, banks are tightening these parameters. Instead of financing a commercial loan over twenty-five years, they may only want to do a fifteen-year amortization. That will raise your monthly payments and hinder your cash flow more than necessary.

Another important question is this: How painless and fast will the lender make the financing approval for you? By now, you will have noticed that's a theme to which I return again and again: Your time is valuable. Time means money. A small business owner should not have to endure the tortures of the damned just because a banker can't give you a quick yes or no, and instead gives you a horribly drawn-out maybe. That can be a painful process; your anxiety will run high. It's not a fun experience.

At the most, it shouldn't take more than a couple of weeks to get a thumbs up or thumbs down from a commercial lender, and this is even in the small business lending arena, where I've heard (and you probably have, too) horror stories about SBA loans taking six months to get approved or closed. It should *never* take that long.

Unfortunately, it's the buyer's choice of lender that determines the time, not the SBA or the SBA loan process. That's why I emphasize that you don't want to be somebody's guinea pig. You can avoid that by asking outright what kind of loans the lender specializes in. Does the commercial lender *do* small business loans regularly? You should get a clear and reassuring affirmative. If not, keep walking.

You want to deal with direct lenders, people who lend their own funds. Make sure that you're not just dealing with a mortgage broker who is representing himself as a lender, whereas in fact all he is doing is brokering your deal to someone else.

There are also hybrid lenders, who often will lend some of their money but may actually partner with someone else. The bottom line is that you get the terms you are seeking or close to them. It doesn't really matter which commercial lender you choose, as long as you are dealing with someone who is reputable.

By the way, you'll notice that I haven't mentioned "what's your rate?" as one of the first questions to ask. That's because all reputable commercial lenders are going to be within a very close range, which has recently been within twenty-five to seventy-five basis points maximum. However, small business owners and their advisers have been conditioned or trained to ask about what I call "the lowest common denominator" (or variable) first, which is the interest rate. The reason they ask it is because they want to make sure they're getting a *fair* rate, and that's perfectly understandable and fine. However, that consideration is fairly minute in comparison to all these other variables or factors. You need to attend to the other variables involved in getting a loan first. If you focus solely on the interest rate, you might not find lenders who are good prospects in many ways including competitive rates.

In many cases, you will find it better to have a slightly higher rate if the loan payment terms are longer and you only have to put down half or a third as much, and it may also pay if you are receiving a much quicker approval process and/or you're dealing with somebody who has figured out a way to get your deal done in the first place.

Those are all factors to consider. You can get such service and still get an interest rate well within the market.

It's that way with many services, and probably for you too in your own business or profession. For the privilege of going to the best dentist in town, many people will gladly pay a bit more. No question. If you're the cheapest at what you do, that's a race to the bottom you probably can't afford. I heard it put another way once: You can't get speed, price, and quality all at once; pick two of the three, and be happy. "Buying" a commercial loan is no different.

Generalists vs. Specialists

Human nature often leads us to trust and continue dealing with our current banker for one-stop shopping. That is normal. But it doesn't mean that's the best and smartest thing to do. As much as we may like one-stop shopping, when the bank tries to do it all, it often is lacking in personalization, customization, and expertise.

Banks tend to be generalists and traditional-minded, doing everything conventionally and in what I call an ordinary fashion. You probably don't think of your small business as ordinary, so you should expect that your lender not treat you that way either.

Specialists will be far more likely to come up with financing solutions that will work for you. Prior to the Great Recession, a lot of people in the financial world wanted to be all things to all people. As generalists, they tried to deal with situations outside their expertise. It got lenders in a whole lot of trouble, and in many ways made the recession even worse.

In the recent commercial lending environment, where banks have been under increased regulatory pressure to reduce their commercial real estate exposure, a lot of bankers think they can just go ahead and do SBA loans because it involves mitigating their lending risks. Many are certainly willing to try it. However, SBA lending is a very specialized area of finance that requires a tremendous amount of knowledge. Small business owners really need to be careful that they're dealing with somebody who can do the job right. A commercial lender should produce testimonials that he has done these types of commercial loans effectively and often. Specialization is key to growth in the newly emerging economy, and you only want to deal with experts. This is of crucial importance in your business and in your choice of commercial lenders.

There's an old adage about banks: They give you an umbrella when it's sunny outside and take it away when it starts to rain. Bankers get a lot of criticism because they tend to be very conservative, not very creative, and extremely slow moving, but that's really a criticism of the status quo, and of generalists overall. We are in a new economy and it's often the specialists—those who move fast and decide quickly—who will excel. Small business owners like you or your clients tend to understand that intuitively.

Nonbank lenders are often specialists. They often focus on niche products and loan options for certain property types. There are some lenders out there who only do gas-station/convenience-store financing, for instance, and I know a commercial lender fairly well who only wants to lend to veterinarians.

My company prefers multipurpose properties, such as office buildings and warehouses, but we also tend to lend increasingly on specialized property types such as limited-service hotels, restaurants, day-care facilities, auto-repair shops, assisted-living facilities, and even marinas. Those are the types of properties in which nonbank lenders can specialize. That's what makes them stand out as the experts in the commercial properties they finance.

We once had a loan officer who focused almost exclusively on Golden Corral franchisee properties. We have had a similar experience with Culver's restaurants, and these days, we seem to finance a lot of the flagged hotel brands such as Country Inn and Suites, Best Western, Holiday Inn Express, Hampton Inn, Comfort Inn, Residence Inn, and Staybridge Suites. These brands came to realize that we knew a lot about their particular projects and therefore like working with us over many others.

A specialist can often be more creative with your financing because of a greater familiarity with particular loan products and property types. Once a lender knows all the mechanics of the procedures and has mastered the specialty, he can focus on finding financing solutions for every client. It allows a more personal approach to commercial real estate financing.

Specialists also can move much faster and be more efficient in underwriting an approval. In my company, we're specialists in commercial real estate financing. We do not finance business acquisitions, for instance, even though I've done plenty such loans in the past. Because we're specialists and experts in one particular loan type, we can be much faster and much more efficient. We're not trying to do other types of lending which would distract us from our primary objective.

Construction Loans

Construction loans are a very specialized type of commercial financing. It's an area that has been hit especially hard over the last few years by this new regulatory environment. The regulators, probably rightfully so, have found that many construction loans went "bad" much more so than "regular" property acquisition loans.

There are many additional risks involved in the commercial construction lending process. You have more fingers in the pie. So, again, you want specialists who can show you the projects they have done, the general contractors they've worked with, the satisfied clients they have, and so forth. A specialist in commercial construction loans will have the experience needed to work accurately, systematically, and efficiently, simplifying the process for all involved. A specialist will have handled such loans many times and is unlikely to make many mistakes.

Banks might offer a construction loan, but if it's not one of their core competencies, you would be wise to steer clear of them because any number of issues could arise to slow your progress and ultimately your project. We probably have 40 percent to 50 percent of our current projects involving some element of construction (either ground-up or renovations), and we have done hundreds of commercial construction projects over the years. Virtually all of them have had change orders that altered the costs from what was proposed up front. In every commercial construction project that we do above a certain dollar amount, we always include what's called a "construction contingency," which is to account for change orders and issues that inevitably come up.

Construction loans often are necessary, however, to bring a property in line with your vision. Oftentimes, it's the best buy for you too because you can renovate a property into your image more cheaply than you can build from the ground up. However, you need to work with people who are familiar with projects like this. Our parent bank—we're a wholly owned subsidiary of Old Florida National Bank—even has us do all of their construction projects because of our expertise. You really want to work with people who know what they're doing here, because there are so many things that can go wrong in the construction space.

Stretching Your Dollars

In obtaining a commercial real estate loan, keep in mind the concept of strategic capital utilization. In essence, this means stretching every dollar as far as you can. In other words, you want to maximize your return for every dollar. Small business owners understand this intuitively in how they run their businesses. They are monitoring their invoices. They are monitoring their expenses. They are monitoring their cash balances in all their accounts. It's how they succeed, but for some reason that instinct often disappears when a banker asks for 30 percent down for a commercial loan. A lot of times, the small business owner gulps and just accepts it.

Commercial real estate investors, particularly people who do this for a living, always look at the particular metric of cash-on-cash return. Ideally you want to get the highest cash-on-cash return that you possibly can. For every dollar that you put in, you want to maximize the return you can get for that dollar. It may work for Sam Zell, a famous real estate investor, or Donald Trump, or any of those guys, but, it also needs to apply for the typical small business owner.

My business partner, Geof, and I are minority investors in a company that purchased a commercial office building back in 2003. The first property we considered had a purchase price of $5.4 million, and four different loan options were considered: two ordinary commercial bank loans, a loan from an insurance company, and a SmartChoice® Commercial Loan. These options were carefully and objectively considered, and the SmartChoice® loan was determined to be the most beneficial option with the highest return on

The following tables are the actual calculations performed for a 2003 transaction in which Geof and I were minority investors. Four loan options were considered, and the SmartChoice® Commercial Loan won out because of its high cash-on-cash return.

Actual 2003 Loan Proposal Options
$5.4 million Purchase Price & Appraisal

Lender	Loan Amount	Equity	Term	Amortization	Rate	Monthly Payment	Fees (Points/ Origination)	Guarantees	Prepayment Penalty	DSC
▮	$4,320,000 (80%)	1,080,000 (20%)	10 years	25 years	10 year Treasury + 180 bp = 5.70 fixed for 10 years	$27,047	None	None – except carve outs for fraud and environmental	3-4 year lockout Yield maintenance thereafter Assumable	1.30 X Maintenance
Mercantile Commercial Capital, LLC	$3,560,000 1st 1,300,000 2nd $4,860,000 (90%)	$540,000 (10%)	25 years 20 years 24 years blend	25 years 20 years 24 years blend	5 year Libor + 275 = 5.90 – fixed 5 years 5.94% fixed for 20 yrs 5.91 blend Blended 9 years fixed	$22,720 9,269 $31,989	$17,800 9,750 $27,550	Limited – pro rata by principal partners	10.9 .. 1% 20% allowable annually w/o penalty Assumable	1.25 X Qualifying No Maintenance
▮	$4,320,000 (80%)	$1,080,000 (20%)	Up to 10 years	20 years	a) Variable @ 3.80 b) Fixed 5 year 5.73 7 year 6.27 10 year 6.78	$25,725 $31,626 7 year	$21,600	Yes- amount and terms TBD	a) No b) Yes-TBD	1.40 X Maintenance
▮	$3,780,000 (70%)	$1,620,000 (30%)	10 years	25 years	10 year Treasury + 200 bp = 5.9% Fixed 10 years	$24,124	$18,900	Non-Recourse	Yield Maintenance Fixed full 10 years	TBD

Return on Investment Calculation*
(Based on $5.4 million building and land purchase price)

	▮	MCC	▮	▮
Present Rent Payment	$591,000	$591,000	$591,000	$591,000
Proposed Debt Service	$324,564	$383,868	$379,512	$289,488
Net Cash Flow Savings	$266,436	$207,132	$211,488	$301,512
Plus Acquired Rental Income	$268,000	$268,000	$268,000	$268,000
Less Property Expenses	($325,433)	($325,433)	($325,433)	($325,433)
Net Cash Flow	$209,003	$149,699	$154,055	$244,079
Investors Equity	$1,080,000	$540,000	$1,080,000	$540,000
Return %	19.35%	27.72%	14.26%	15.07%

*The return percentage calculated is the cash-on-cash return – the metric used by the most successful commercial real estate investors to determine whether a deal or project will be profitable, and to what degree. Generally the higher the cash-on-cash return, the better the project.

investment. We ultimately purchased a less expensive building, and this original analysis convinced us that the SmartChoice® loan was the right choice. Even though lenders aren't eligible for Smart-Choice/504 financing, this is how I can say that I've used the very loan product that I recommend for other small business owners. Not many (probably not ANY) other commercial lenders could say the same.

This is why I'm such a strong advocate of the SmartChoice® Commercial Loan, the SBA 504 loan. It allows small business owners to have a down payment that's a third to half as much as a bank ordinarily requires. With these commercial loans, small business owners can keep so much more of their precious capital on hand to grow their business. Stretching every dollar is the smart approach.

Planting Your Flag

People tend to buy for emotional reasons and they justify their decision with logical ones. They've received good terms for their down payment, for example, or a favorable amortization. They received an incredible fixed interest rate and a quick approval. Those are all logical reasons to go for it, but we have to understand that there is an emotional piece in all of this.

It's tough to be a small business owner. It is one of the loneliest things you can do. It's not easy to do it. If it were, you'd have a far greater number of successful entrepreneurs out there. Often you are putting out fires all day long. Things seem to be going crazy a lot of the time. Many people want no part of that kind of life. It's been said that entrepreneurs live a few years as no one else would (working crazy hours and putting up with tremendous stresses), so they can live many years as no one else will (care-free and prosperous). Those who do endure the struggles will come to feel that they deserve something. You've arrived, and it's about time that you plant your own flag. It's kind of like that story I told earlier about Michael Dell wanting the three flags in front of his building.

All those nuts-and-bolts financial considerations are crucial, of course, but the emotional aspects play a huge role, and I've rarely ever heard an ordinary banker discuss this. Buying a "home" for your business is an emotional journey, and you want a commercial lender who will encourage you along the way, not throw obstacles in your path. It's important that your lender help you find a yes rather than lead you to no's.

More Questions to Ask a Lender

Have you worked with many other small businesses?

It's important that you work with a commercial lender who understands businesses like yours. Big-time corporate lenders find it difficult to sympathize with the struggles of an entrepreneur, and they are likely to give preferential treatment to their larger corporate clients.

What's your experience in my industry or with my type of commercial property?

It is definitely a plus if the lender has experience working with other borrowers in your specific industry or who bought similar types of commercial property. A lender who has a track record of working with borrowers like you will be able to anticipate the questions and concerns you'll have.

There are a lot of property types that banks traditionally don't want to finance or make it more difficult to approve, and you should know that going in. A lot of banks do not like hotels. They may not like to finance restaurants, or day cares, or auto-repair shops, or gas station/convenience stores. Pretty much anything that's not a multipurpose property is going to cause some element of consternation on the part of an ordinary banker.

What is the time frame for this commercial loan process?

Each lender may have a different time frame for processing your preapproval and commercial loan application. You don't want to deal with a lender who won't make your loan a priority. You should make your expectations clear up front, and come to an understand-

Questions to Ask Commercial Lenders

Many small business owners make the mistake of believing that a lender is a lender is a lender...and they end up working with their current banker simply because it seems most convenient. Many bankers are very competent, but certainly not all of them. Moreover, most banks offer many different financial products but don't specialize in any one thing, which can lead to a poor and bumpy experience. The following list of questions will help you weed through potential commercial lenders to find the right one for your project.

- Have you worked with many other small businesses?
- What's your experience in my industry or with my type of commercial property?
- What is the timeframe for this commercial loan process?
- What is your typical loan-to-value?
- Is this loan assumable?
- Are there any financial covenants?
- Do your loans have balloon payments?
- Can I talk to past clients of yours as references?

This list is by no means finite, so feel free to modify these questions and/or add some that you come up with. Every commercial real estate project is unique, and you deserve the proper time, attention, effort, and resources to get the job done right.

ing with your lender as to what is a reasonable time frame for your loan to be approved or not.

What is your typical loan-to-value?

Loan-to-value (LTV) is a calculation that divides the loan amount by the appraised value of the property you want to buy. For example, let's say the property you're considering costs $500,000 and you are putting down $100,000. Your LTV ratio would be 80 percent. The amount to be financed is $400,000, which is 80 percent of $500,000.

Typically, a lower LTV (higher equity injection or down payment) will enable you to get a lower interest rate. For example, many banks will require as much as 25 percent to 35 percent down. This lessens their risk and makes them more comfortable with giving you a competitive interest rate.

Some loan programs (such as the SBA 504 loan) deal with loan-to-cost (LTC) rather than LTV. This means that the lender is financing a portion of the total project cost (construction/acquisition, renovations/tenant improvements, equipment, soft costs, and closing costs) as opposed to the appraised value of the property. This is extremely beneficial to you as a borrower because your out-of-pocket costs (or capital required) will go down dramatically.

Most of the time, however, a lender is going to deal with loan-to-value, using the lesser of the appraised value or purchase price. Let's say you were able to negotiate the purchase of a million-dollar property for only $800,000. The bank is traditionally going to finance it only on the $800,000.

Is this loan assumable?

If you think you might sell your property one day, an assumable loan will let you transfer the remainder of the commercial loan balance to the new owner. You always want to have an exit strategy, and this will be a great selling point down the road, especially in an era of interest rates that are higher than today's.

If you do ordinary commercial financing with a bank, the loan probably will not be assumable. You don't have this issue with a SmartChoice® Commercial Loan. Those are traditionally assumable.

Are there any financial covenants?

Beware of lenders who want to include many financial covenants in your loan. A lot of people don't understand that this means they deem you pretty risky, and they want to be able to check up on you to make sure you're able to pay back your loan. Avoid such covenants if at all possible. You many have language in your loan agreement, for example, that says you have to maintain that debt service coverage ratio annually, and that if you get below that, the lender has the ability to call your loan. You may have to maintain a certain debt-to-worth ratio as well. The fewer the covenants, the less lender micromanagement you'll have to deal with.

Do your loans have balloon payments?

Some lenders will give you a good deal on your loan but include a balloon payment. This means that you may enjoy very low monthly payments for three or five years, but after a set amount of time you'll be hit with a rather large lump-sum payment of the remaining principal. That is called a balloon payment, and it is not something you will encounter with a SmartChoice® Commercial Loan. Balloon payments are often so large that business owners must refinance the debt with another lender, which means more closing costs and fees. (I will discuss balloon payments in detail in the next chapter.)

Can I talk to past clients of yours as references?

To learn about a lender, the best people to ask are those with whom the lender has worked in the past. Try to pinpoint clients whose situation was similar to yours: the same industry, type of property, or some other common area. That way, you'll get some idea of what your experience will be. When you talk to past clients, you will want to know if they were treated fairly, if the lender was helpful with the application and paperwork, if the loan process was completed in a reasonable time frame, and whether they would work with that lender again.

CLIENT SPOTLIGHT

JEFF CURRAN, TEAM CURRAN MARTIAL ARTS ACADEMY
CRYSTAL LAKE, IL

Jeff Curran is a professional Mixed Martial Arts (MMA) fighter and owner of Team Curran Martial Arts Academy. His training facility is one of the largest in the world and is open to the public, with classes ranging from beginner to advanced levels incorporating different types of fighting styles. Jeff, known as "the Big Frog" in MMA circles, and the rest of Team Curran train at his gym in the Chicagoland area, and compete at the national and international levels in Ultimate Fighting Championship (UFC) and other similar organizations. Mercantile Capital Corporation helped Jeff purchase his training facility with a SmartChoice® Commercial Loan.

Your nickname is "The Big Frog." Why is that?
Back in the late 1990s I was training at a gym out in Salt Lake City. Some of my Brazilian friends started saying that the way I was training—some of the drills I was doing—made me look like a big frog on the mat. It just so happened that I had a tattoo of a frog on my back, so they started calling me "the Big Frog" in Portuguese. Everyone else started asking what they were calling me, and they told them, and that was it. The name just stuck.

How did you get involved in martial arts? What age were you?

The first time I ever took a class in any martial arts was when I was five years old. My brother was a few years older than I was, and he kind of got uninterested after a short while. My mom pulled both of us, but I always kept an interest [in it], so she signed me back up with different park-district-type things, and my grandpa started training me in boxing when I was around eleven years old. I started boxing with him, and I was wrestling full-time for school, so I was always involved in something similar to martial arts, some kind of one-on-one combat.

I played ice hockey most of my life too, so it was all kind of related—you know, a little bit more rough than most sports.

The biggest transition was in 1993 when Royce Gracie fought in the Ultimate Fighting Championship. It was a pay-per-view sixteen-man tournament, and everybody came out and did no-rules, no-time-limit fighting, and as soon as I saw that, I was sold. I never looked back. I started looking for fight promoters who were starting up shows, and started getting into it. Little by little I became known as one of the better guys, and then eventually there was a ranking system and a weight class and the sport began to organize a little more. Shortly after that, I established myself in the top ten, and I've been there ever since.

Ultimate Fighting is such a physical and aggressive sport.
What's the worst injury you've gotten?
I blocked a kick when I was over in Japan, and my forearm
bone split in half and almost protruded through my skin. I
had to get a plate put on and screwed back together. That's
been the one that's stuck with me and given me the most
problems over time, but I think the most dangerous one
I had was a facial injury from taking a bad punch. The
doctors did a CAT scan and estimated it was, like, 15,000
fractures to my orbital area. It just completely shattered—
no disfiguration or anything like that—and I wasn't able to
really stand up or walk for a few days, and I had to take it
easy and wait until things started settling down. I just took
a really hard punch, and that was probably my most scary
moment.

I come out of some of my roughest fights ever that are just
fifteen minutes straight of back-and-forth war—and I get
bumps, bruises, black eyes, bloody noses, and cuts—but
the serious injuries really are few and far between. I've had
some bad knee injuries and things like that from training
and whatnot, but for the most part there's something about
it that keeps me moving forward and taking that risk. It's
kind of like a big stock investment, you know.

How much time do you spend preparing for your fights?
A normal training camp would probably put me at about
six hours a day of actual physical training, sometimes a little
bit more, and I do that five to six days a week.

The diet's tight. To give you an example, breakfast is one hardboiled egg, one hardboiled egg white, and a little bit of protein mix. The next meal is a can of turkey or a can of tuna and a half a slice of bread, and then at night, I'll have maybe four ounces of meat with some asparagus or something like that. I start eating very little, and I take my multivitamins, and I take my pre- and post-workout proteins. That's pretty much my diet going into a fight. That kind of a meal plan is probably about three weeks away from a fight. Six or eight weeks out from a fight, my portion sizes are bigger. I'll eat some chicken. I'll still be eating a little bit of cheese. I have to make sure I'm eating healthy more than anything because I'm training so hard that the calories just come off. As long as I'm not putting in deep-fried foods and a lot of real high sugars and fructose and stuff like that, my body's fine.

I recently watched an episode of a TV show called TapouT. Have you seen it?

I'm actually on one of the episodes. One of them featured my fighter, Sunshine. I'll also be in the upcoming season, in the corner with my cousin, Pat Curran. They're doing this blood-line thing, following families involved in mixed martial arts (MMA). *TapouT* is actually one of my sponsors, and they've been with me for a long time. I'm glad they're doing this show. It's a great way of documenting a fighter's new beginning. I've been lucky enough to have been on the show as a coach and also as a promoter.

*Why do you think Ultimate Fighting is becoming so
mainstream and popular?*

Our demographic is very densely populated with eighteen-
to thirty-five-year-old males. Where there are young guys,
there are young girls, and where there are young girls there
are more guys, and it's just grown. They like watching
the fights, and each of the fighters has something unique
that attracts people, and the marketing does a good job of
playing up all of that.

From an actual fight standpoint, you've got two guys risking
it all standing face-to-face. It's not like you're trying to just
ride out a fight, like in boxing where the judges can make a
decision in the end. We're going for broke, and it makes for
exciting entertainment.

*Would you like either of your children to get into the
family business?*

Yeah, I want them to know the business. I want them to
become good trainers. I want them to train and learn jujitsu
and hopefully go out and do jujitsu tournaments and be
successful that way, but I can't really picture my son fighting
just yet because right now he's just this little guy who's so
sweet and fragile. I just can't even picture it right now, and
I don't want anything to ever happen to him. So right now
him fighting isn't even really in my thoughts.

Now, since all your success, what has changed in your life?

Well, my gym keeps growing. It keeps getting bigger and
bigger. Everything I do seems to turn into something else,

and I have to make smart decisions, as far as investing goes. I have to watch my money a little bit. The bigger you grow, the farther down you can fall, and I have to kind of pace myself a little bit to make sure I make wise choices. I can't just act on impulse like I used to.

I've always been responsible, but when I'm the kind of guy that gets an idea I just go with it. Sometimes I step back and realize that maybe I went a little too far. I need to back up a little bit. When you start playing with bigger deals, you have to slow down and really weigh the pros and cons, or you'll end up crumbling.

Speaking of bigger deals, how did you get involved with my company, Mercantile Capital Corporation (MCC) for the financing of your new facility?
I was turned down by, like, nine banks. I was going around from bank to bank, trying to get financing for this project. I was going to buy some land from a few of my students and build a mega training center, and I kept getting shot down. I just couldn't get the financing in place. I didn't show enough growth. Even though I had positive growth, it wasn't enough. This went on for about six months to a year. Finally, I got connected with an agent named Donetta [Shuster], and we clicked right away. She just started going to town for me, and she came across MCC, and you were willing to hear my story and look a little bit deeper into what I was trying to do. As soon as you guys did that, you realized that it was definitely a doable deal and you could help me get financing for my building.

You got me approved to build on some open land, but it turns out the land I was looking at was a year or so away from being zoned for what I wanted to do, and that was going to slow things up too much. So, I started looking again, and shortly after that I found a place. MCC was the one organization that stepped in and said, "Hey, this is something we can do, and we think that this guy's got the strength to support the deal."

Working with us, did you have any problems? How helpful were we?

You really made it easy on me. I told Donetta afterward that I could not imagine doing this with anybody else. There's no way. I just couldn't picture it. If there was any more stress along the way, it probably would have killed me, and everybody [at MCC] just made it easy. Everybody communicated with me, and that's really important. I respected that, and I still do, and I'll absolutely go back [to you].

I have to increase my enrollment a lot to make this a profitable experience. It'll pay the bills, but I need to grow my school. I hope to put an addition onto the building that I purchased. I have a good chunk of land, so I can always just add on. You know, the sport has been really popular, and it's starting to spin off things like nutritional products, so I recently started a nutritional supplement company, and I'll probably be fighting for the next ten years or so, at least until I get too old to do it.

What would you say is your favorite city to fight in?

I'd have to say Vegas. I've been to Japan. I've fought out of Chicago. There are some great fans in Chicago. The thing about Vegas is that you just feel like you're there to fight. You know, everybody's there on a vacation. You're staying at the hotel you're fighting in, and everyone in the hotel is there for the fight. It's just real motivating.

Everybody flew there on their own dollar and they're real fans, you know. You're fighting for people who are familiar with you and what you do, and that's a little more motivating than fighting in front of a bunch of heckling guys that don't know anything about what's going on.

If you could to talk to other entrepreneurs who want to own their commercial property, would you recommend MCC?

I would definitely recommend MCC, and the biggest thing I'd say is don't let anybody tell you it can't be done. I was told that from the beginning, and I just kept moving forward. MCC took the time to hear my story, which was more than some banks did. But you still had to decide whether or not you believed in me. You did believe in me, and I imagine you'd believe in other people, too.

CHAPTER FIVE

Obtaining the Best Loan

In embracing change, entrepreneurs ensure social and economic stability.
—GEORGE GILDER

*Ninety-nine percent of the failures come from people
who have the habit of making excuses.*
—GEORGE WASHINGTON CARVER

Once you have chosen your lender, you can look more closely at the types of financing that are available for the purchase of commercial real estate. A good lender will help you explore several loan options.

Conventional Commercial Loans

Conventional or traditional commercial loans are called that for a reason: they're the most common type. Banks provide most of them. Usually they are only used to finance commercial properties or equipment, and they are often used to refinance existing commercial mortgages. You don't see a lot of conventionally financed business acquisitions, for instance.

Typically, a conventional commercial loan will have a fixed rate, not a floating or variable one. However, fixed rates here are different from those of the residential world. Fixed rates on commercial property or equipment are typically fixed only for a set period of time. With residential mortgages, the fixed rate is usually in place for the entire length of the amortization. That's not generally the case with conventional commercial loans.

For example, it's very common to have a three-, five-, seven-, or even sometimes a ten-year fixed rate on a commercial mortgage, and then, at the end of that time period, the rate will reset. It may become a floating rate, or a balloon payment may come due on the loan, and therefore it will need to be refinanced, either with the same lender or another (incurring new costs and fees in the process). The amortization for conventional commercial financing is usually for monthly payments over a period of fifteen or twenty years. The term of the loan itself may be less than that, and that's usually relating to the fixed interest rate and/or the presence of a ballooning note. You'll learn more about balloon payments soon in this chapter.

Right now, it's very common for a conventional loan to require a 20 percent to 35 percent down payment, and a lot of times, the small business owner must pay the closing costs out-of-pocket. These include expenses such as loan origination fees, the commercial appraisal fee, the title insurance, environmental reports, surveys, attorney's fees, and so on. Those soft costs can amount to several percent of the project costs, and they are not typically financed as part of the loan. Borrowers often don't think about how those costs will affect their available cash.

It's often said that cash flow is the lifeblood of business. So whenever you can include any of the costs associated with the financing into the loan itself, you can preserve more of your capital to operate or grow your business, or at least maintain the flexibility to do so. That's the principle of strategic capital utilization, and a lot of small business owners don't take that into consideration for their commercial property financing. They consider it every day as they run their businesses, of course, but usually not for their major purchase of commercial property. A lot of times, they just do whatever their banker tells them they need to do and settle for what the banker leads them to believe is just the way it's normally done. This is trusting an authority figure too much.

However, that's not necessarily the way it's always done. Just because something is normal doesn't mean it has to apply to you. You probably think of your business as anything but normal. So, the less money you have to pay out of pocket, the better off you will be.

Beware Those Balloons

If your loan has a provision for you to make a balloon payment, all the principal balance will come due at a designated time. Let's say you've recently gotten a conventional commercial loan. It typically would have a five-year fixed rate and require a 25 percent down payment. You paid for some closing costs out-of-pocket, so you had to come up with 28 percent of the total project costs in cash, and you have an attractive five-year interest rate.

At the end of five years, however, you will have to get a new loan. A lot of people think that getting a new loan with their existing lender will be easy, a given even, but that's not necessarily the case. I've seen many examples of situations where a particular industry falls out of favor with a lender, and therefore that lender has no interest in renewing your loan at the end of the initial term. If that happens to you, you will have to go to another lender and refinance the principal balance, and whether renewing or refinancing, you're going to have costs associated with getting a new commercial loan. Small business owners often don't factor that in when they consider the provisions of a conventional loan. They don't realize that getting a loan with a balloon payment is basically just deferring some costs of the loan into the future, but those costs eventually will catch up with them.

I remember a situation when I was working at GE Capital, in which a large general contractor in the Southeast had gone bankrupt. For a number of years after that, GE Capital would not lend *any* more money to *any* general contractors. It didn't matter where you were in the country or world. GE had lost a lot of money with that one contractor and just said, "Forget it, we're out of that sector entirely." They didn't care how impressive the debt service coverage was, or how favorable the loan-to-value was. No general contractor was going to get a loan at that time from GE. I had a general contractor client whose GE loan was coming due for a balloon payment, but there was no way that GE was going to refinance my client's loan. He had to go elsewhere.

There have been numerous cases in recent years in which borrowers have been pushed out of lenders' portfolios for a variety of reasons. Lenders have been under intense regulatory pressure not to do commercial real estate loans, particularly for certain special-purpose property types. When those balloon payments have come due, small business owners have had to *hope* they can get refinancing with another lender, and "hope," dare I say, is a pretty poor business strategy. Lenders are trying to protect themselves and minimize their own risk, but unfortunately the inverse of that is that the risk rises for the typical small business owner.

The balloon payment will add an element of uncertainty to your business, and a lot of people don't think about that at first. In fact, most conventional commercial loan officers tend to gloss over it, and you'll get too far down the rabbit hole toward your closing to turn back. I've seen that happen many times to small business owners. It's unfortunate. They're not given the spectrum of details so they don't anticipate what will happen in five years, and even when they do, the stress and uncertainty are certainly *not* what they bargained for.

Covenants and Call Provisions

Covenants and call provisions are very similar to balloons. In order to keep your loan current with your lender, you may be required to maintain a certain debt-to-worth ratio, or you may be required to maintain a certain debt service coverage ratio. If you don't, the lender has the right to call your loan, which typically means that you must pay your loan off in cash or refinance it, perhaps with another lender. This situation often occurs with a very short time frame, frequently within a few months, and so that can cause major problems for a typical small business.

This is lender micromanagement. It's a way for the bank to mitigate its risk. It may want you to maintain a 1.2 times debt service coverage ratio, and in your last fiscal year, you had a 0.8 times debt service coverage ratio. That sets off alarms that maybe it's only a matter of time before you can no longer make the loan payments. The bank will want to push you out, before *it* gets hurt.

As an advocate for small business owners, I can help avoid such hurdles. I do understand the lenders' perspective, and often these covenants are part of their loan policy. Covenants are quite common, and the bank may be unwilling to even talk about negotiating them out of a deal, particularly in the recent economic climate. Nonetheless, you should certainly try to do so if you are going for conventional financing. Just understand you may not succeed because the lenders are dotting their *i*'s and crossing their *t*'s. They're trying to make up today for the mistakes of the recent past.

Transfer Requirements

Loan agreements frequently include language requiring the small business owner to transfer his or her business checking accounts or other operating accounts to the new lender. Unless you're really unhappy with your present bank where you have all your accounts and numerous monthly payments are already linked to those accounts, you're probably not going to want to do that. It's not a lot of fun to have to move all your accounts to another bank and change over all those recurring payments, especially when you're just trying to get a commercial loan. It's not quite like getting a lobotomy, but it's close. Yet, the lenders may try to require that. It makes good economic sense for the bank, and it earns a commission for the loan officer, but it may not make a lot of practical sense for you as a small business owner, so you have to be careful with things like that.

Those in the banking world have operated for centuries on a very simple principle: They want to hold your money and pay you a little bit so they can turn around and lend it out at higher rates than they are paying you. So, every bank wants as much of your business as it can get. They want to do more than just make a commercial loan to you if they consider you a healthy small business; they also want to have all your business accounts. Some banks offer insurance products and investment products, and they'll want to do as much of that business as possible. They're going to want to make money off you in any way they can. If you have an account with a cash balance of $150,000, that's a nice chunk of business for most banks.

I firmly agree with the adage that you shouldn't keep all your eggs in one basket. A small business owner should want to have operating accounts at a couple different banks, maybe a commercial loan with one lender, and a line of credit with another. That's what I encourage, but it's not what a bank would encourage, so be careful. If your credit is strong, the bank is going to want everything that it can get its hands on, and that doesn't always make the most sense for you.

How Long Until Closing?

A commercial real estate contract typically is going to be written so that it takes 60 to 120 days to close the loan. Banks these days— again, because of the regulatory environment and the scrutiny that they are under—are going to be operating much more slowly than they ever have, and they weren't terribly fast to begin with. If you're dealing with a generalist bank that only does conventional lending, its loan committee may only meet once or twice a month. That's going to bog down the process, and you may have difficulty settling your deal if it takes too long to close.

A commercial loan specialist can expedite the process. Think about how long you might wait in the office of a family physician versus the length of your wait in a specialist's office. The latter is likely to have a far more streamlined schedule because of the narrower focus.

So What's BEST for You?

It's not uncommon, then, for commercial lenders to emphasize loan products designed to be advantageous to themselves but not nearly as suitable for you.

The amount of the down payment, for example, decreases their risk, but it ties up a lot of your capital, as do those soft and closing costs that you pay out-of-pocket. And you will get no immediate return on this invested capital. The assets you lock up in a down payment could be better used elsewhere, and that brings us back, once again, to the principle of strategic capital utilization. If the bank is requiring you to put in two or three times more than necessary as a down payment, you must consider the cost of the lost opportunity. How might that money be better invested for an immediate return? Could you instead purchase machinery to improve operations and your bottom line? Could you use the money to hire someone whose skills will bring in far more revenue than what you pay in salary? You might use the money saved to start that marketing plan that you've been wanting to do for years.

There's a lot you can do to stretch your dollars, and that's why you don't want to put as much down as most conventional lenders will require. You want to closely monitor your cash flow, of course, so a commercial loan with a longer payback period will also leave you more money for today.

These are good reasons not to go down the traditional path when seeking a commercial loan product. My philosophy is that if you do what the crowd does, then you tend to get what's ordinary and what's conventional. You "regress to the mean," which is the average, and the average is mediocrity at best. If you want to position your business to do something extraordinary, you have to do things that are different from the norm.

From an economic standpoint, think of it this way: It's going to be a lot harder for that small business owner to create jobs and to really grow his business and profits if so much of his excess cash went into servicing debt, whether through higher monthly payments, or a balloon that forced him to refinance in a few years' time, or a higher down payment. Traditional bank financing has, in many respects, thwarted the growth of the small business sector and that's a shame for us all.

SMARTCHOICE® COMMERCIAL LOAN STRUCTURE

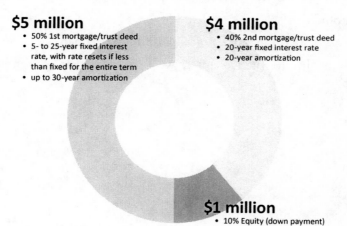

$5 million
- 50% 1st mortgage/trust deed
- 5- to 25-year fixed interest rate, with rate resets if less than fixed for the entire term
- up to 30-year amortization

$4 million
- 40% 2nd mortgage/trust deed
- 20-year fixed interest rate
- 20-year amortization

$1 million
- 10% Equity (down payment)

The SmartChoice® Commercial Loan

There's a better way, and it's readily available. For years I have been beating the drum for the SBA's 504 loan program. The down payment is much smaller than with a traditional loan, and you can have far longer to pay the loan back, which means more money stays in your pocket. With a twenty-, twenty-five- or thirty-year term, you're going to see much lower monthly payments. The only collateral is the owner-occupied commercial property you are buying, and you get a great interest rate, far below the prevailing market rates, with no balloon payments.

You may well never hear about this loan from bankers. It's not as easy for them to deliver, and they're going to get paid less (as we discussed earlier). Yet, you see plenty of advertising campaigns from bankers talking about how they only offer what's in the best interest of their customers. If that were the case, then something as simple as the SBA 504 loan would be more widely known all across the country, not just on the West Coast, and it would be more widely used by small business owners like you. It's simply a better, smarter loan product.

We call it the SmartChoice® Commercial Loan, because that's what it is. In the next chapter, we'll take a closer look at all its advantages.

CLIENT SPOTLIGHT

RICHARD AND CAROL KENDALL, CULVER'S RESTAURANTS
CEDAR RAPIDS, IOWA

Richard and Carol Kendall decided to get into franchising with Culver's in 1998, and quickly had two locations up and running successfully in Iowa. The restaurant chain became famous for its frozen custard and butterburgers, and has grown to more than 450 franchises across nineteen states. Mercantile Capital Corporation was able to help the Kendalls with their third location by providing long-term and construction financing.

How did you get started as a husband-and-wife team working in the franchise restaurant business?

Richard: We decided to take another direction in our life. Our children were pretty much grown up. My previous background was in a retail clothing business with my father, and I really enjoyed the aspect of being my own boss. I also worked as a distributor rep with a building products company. It was a good job, good company, but decisions were made somewhere else in the country, and you weren't directly responsible for what happened half the time. So we kind of looked around and decided we wanted to move back into something where we're in control of our destiny.

Carol: I sold auto glass for a company in Dubuque, Iowa. I did a lot of traveling, and I had a really nice job, because basically I handed out pens and paper and took clients out to lunch. For some reason, I decided to quit taking them out and start serving them, and I think we made a great decision. We work together, Rich and I, very well; and like he says, we can make decisions now that affect our business and our employees and our customers without having to go to someone else and have them make decisions for us. So we're very happy in the industry we're in.

You seem to be part of a trend I've noticed over the last few years. Baby boomers are getting out of corporate America and deciding they want a different career; they want to be their own boss, but maybe they don't want to start something from scratch. Maybe they'd rather buy into sort of a turnkey operation, and I think that's what you have with your Culver's franchises.

Carol: Yeah, I think that's exactly right. If you look around, do your homework, and find a franchise with some great core values and great support. Rich and I knew nothing about running a quick, casual-type restaurant. We had eaten at several Culver's. We liked the concept, so we investigated. We went to several of their sixty-hour courses, and they approved us for a franchise. We knew what we were getting into with them, and the support has always been there from Culver's. They've turned us into some restaurateurs, I guess.

This was your third one that we helped you finance. Rich, you worked in a family-run business for about sixteen years, right?

Richard: That's correct. It took me fifteen years to graduate from college. We started a family and other different things.

Anyway, it was a family-owned business in a small town, and we were making a profit and doing good business, but trends change. The big-box stores came in, and that was when we chose to sell the business and go in a different direction. At that point in time is when I started as a distributor rep.

Did your father have a business while you were growing up?
Richard: Yeah, he did a wide range of different things. He's passed since. He was in the grocery business for twenty-five years, and he was also in the men's retail clothing business for twenty-five years.

I see this regularly with our clients that they had some early childhood or early adult experience with another entrepreneur. Many times, it's a family member.
Richard: We did not have restaurant experience eight years ago, but we had business experience. I try telling my employees and some of the younger people, but it's hard to explain to them. There's a dollar coming in the front door, but twenty-five cents goes to this, thirty cents goes to that, a dime goes to this, and after those costs, this is the amount I have left from that dollar. Too often people go into businesses and think, "Boy, I got a dollar. That's my dollar." Well, it is for a while.

Tell my readers a little bit about the franchise and how you would describe it.

Richard: Culver's is a privately owned company, franchised out of Sauk City, Wisconsin. Presently, they have around 340 units and are continuously opening more. They're basically located in the Midwest from Minnesota and Wisconsin, down through Texas. They've also branched out west to Wyoming and Colorado, east to Ohio, and one just opened in Kentucky. They will also be opening franchises in Arizona. So yeah, they're primarily a Midwest franchise, but they're also spreading out a little bit. They're not jumping into anything without the proper support. Part of their philosophy includes servicing a specific area with several units, such as in Arizona. They've waited for a commitment from several people so there's not just one freestanding unit in the area that has to go it alone.

Tell us about what you guys offer. I know you guys are famous for butterburgers and custard—premium ice cream. You potentially have customers all day long.

Carol: Oh yeah. They certainly come in for desserts. We have a gentleman up at our Hiawatha store who comes in at 10:30 a.m. and the first thing he has is a sundae. That's my kind of meal! When you come in, you can see the custard machine and see the custard being made fresh. We do chocolate and vanilla every day. During the summer months, we have lemon ice which you can add to the custard or have by itself as a cooler; it's neat to see it being made. It's rich and smooth and just a terrific treat.

Richard: For the butterburgers, we use quality ground beef that's never frozen. It's purchased and processed locally in the Midwest. Burgers aren't made until they're ordered, so they're not sitting in a steamer, and we're not just a burger and custard or ice cream place. We also have chicken sandwiches, different types of salads, and a full menu.

Whom do you guys consider your main competition?
Richard: I don't consider us true fast food. We are in the quick-casual restaurant category, so we compete with McDonald's and Burger King and those chains, but we also compete with others in the family-oriented niche, like Applebee's.

I understand that the first restaurant was opened in 1984 by George and Ruth Culver, and that their son, Craig, has taken the ball and run with it.
Richard: Craig and his wife, Leigh, are the co-CEOs. They own, I believe, five corporate stores, located throughout the country. The rest are all franchise-owned, either by single people, such as Carol and myself, or possibly a group. One of the criteria is that the owner is an owner-operator and has a hands-on approach. This fosters pride and consistency among the stores. Our first store was number seventy-four, which we opened in 1999. Our Hiawatha store, which we opened a year and a half later, is number 109 and our most recent one, which we opened with your help in March in Marion, Iowa, is number 320. They're up in the 400s, presently. Hiawatha and Marion are suburbs of Cedar Rapids, and the stores are all within seven miles of

each other, but each one of those stores serves a different demographic.

Richard: The corporate support is important to us, but they give you the freedom to run each individual store along their guidelines. So, it's kind of the best of both worlds. Without their expertise, we can't do things that they can do. They've got the expertise and all the knowledge, so we just feed off that, and when you're in the battlefield, that's where you learn the most.

Let's talk about your project a little bit. I remember getting a phone call from Carol because I think you read an article about us in Franchise Times. *You told me you own the real estate for the previous two franchises. I still come up against resistance sometimes with franchisees about the whole concept of owning the real estate as opposed to leasing a facility when they have an option. To me, it seems like a no-brainer.*

Carol: I was in the real estate business back in Maquoketa, where Rich and I are originally from, and I learned before long that they're just not making any more land. So, if you can own a piece of it, it's better than the rock. We thought if we could purchase the property where our stores are located, make the payments, and support our employees and families, we'd really have an investment at the end.

So how do you market your three locations?
Richard: Well, part of our franchise agreement goes toward a cooperative advertising fund from which the corporate

family produces national TV ads and things like that, which we can't do locally real well. What we do locally is try to advertise not only with local radio and TV, but we also do a lot of ours through churches, schools, etc., to get local involvement from the people that are supporting us. Most of our marketing is done by giving to different fund-raising causes, different schools, and hopefully, we create a mutually beneficial relationship. We support them, and they support us.

Tell me about your fondest memory in business.
Carol: My fondest memory, I would have to say, is when our son and daughter both expressed interest in being involved in the company with us, and our son-in-law is a CPA and is involved with the financial statements, payroll, and things like that.

Richard: I'd also say that my fondest memory is the satisfaction from all of our hard work, whether it was at day one when we started and didn't know anything (and maybe some days still don't!) or in more recent times. We continually learn, but the satisfaction is that we did it. We worked through it. We have had some problems, but our whole team worked together—our managers, sub managers, and our crew members—and they're satisfied about getting the job done. Sure we make mistakes daily, but our biggest thing is how we react to those mistakes and how we do the next time.

To what do you attribute your successes?

Carol: I would say our employees. They are the ones who make the stores what they are today—their smiles, their welcoming attitudes, the stories they bring with them. Customers come in and we call them by name, and it's almost like a family-run business.

Richard: I tell my people, "The customer who comes in the door is the one who pays you. Without that customer, you don't have a job, and you don't get a paycheck. So treat them as you would want to be treated if you walked into their place of business."

How many employees do you have now between the three locations?

Richard: Probably around 150 to 175, and it varies at different times of the year.

Carol: Some are young. There have been several people we hired at fourteen years old who have stayed with us through their college years. We've gotten notes from them and cards from them saying, "Thank you. This is the only job I've ever had all through high school and all through college. We really appreciate the upbringing and the values that you've set forth." But I also remember when we first opened the Edgewood store and I hired a lady who was in her mid-seventies. Three or four months after we were open, she gave us a thank-you note that said, "Thank you for giving me a reason for getting up in the morning," and that was one of the best rewards I think I've ever had in the business.

What are the biggest obstacles you guys have faced?
Richard: Probably the biggest obstacle is people—you know, trying to get them trained properly and retaining them, and the turnover is high. With young people, our number-one priority is their personal success; school and their family life comes first, and we just want to blend in so it's the best for both of us. So, probably the human resource part of it is our biggest obstacle in our industry.

Carol: One of the others, I would have to say, would be our health-care issues. We do offer health care for our full-time employees, and the cost has risen dramatically in the last seven years. It has close to doubled, and that comes right off the bottom line.

What about personal obstacles you have overcome in business?
Carol: When we first started, we basically had to sell everything we had to get up and get going, and it was pretty stressful at times because we were putting all our eggs in one basket. It takes a lot of money to get started in something like this, but you have to commit to it.

Richard: Those first days at Edgewood were very memorable. We opened up in late February—winter in Iowa—basically by word-of-mouth, and it was a fabulous opening. We started out going gangbusters. Our regular hours are 10:30 a.m. till 10 p.m., seven days a week, and we had customers from 10:15 a.m. to 10:30 p.m. It was a rough start. Basically, we were there all but maybe four hours out of a twenty-four-hour day. There were nights we didn't get out of there till 1:30 a.m. and we were back there at 6 a.m. We initially scraped together enough money for the first store. Then we did it for the second, and now we've done it for the third store.

Carol: I'm real happy to have our son involved because if there's a fourth and fifth out there, I think he's going to be a lot more involved. Like Rich says, Florida and Arizona and southern Texas are looking pretty good to us right now.

What have you guys learned in your work experience?
Carol: Well, I've learned that you have to respect your employees, and you have to train them. That's the key to keeping them. Another lesson is to be involved with your community. You really need to be. I handle most of the fund-raising here, and I probably get five to ten contribution letters a day. You really have to pick and choose what and who you donate to. You'd love to be able to give to everything, but you just can't.

You've got to budget things. I am a firm believer in the four-walls marketing theory, where most of your marketing is done right within the four walls of your business and once you get those people in the door, you want to suggestive-sell them. Not only that, but we also do a lot of sampling. We give customers small cups of the flavor of the day, and that's how we sample our product. That way, we're getting that product right to the customer. Cedar Rapids is a great city for festivals and parades, so that's a great way to do marketing, too.

What ultimately made you choose us for financing, and how did we do?

Richard: Well, I think you've kind of got from this conversation that we support our local people and we like them to support us. Our other two loans are through a local branch of a national bank. We had been dealing with them through the whole process for our third store, and there was miscommunication between the local institution and an SBA group that was working with it. Unfortunately, somebody dropped the ball along the line on those two parts. This was well into our procedure for opening and getting going on this store. We were to the point where we had to move forward because we had invested X number of dollars and we just couldn't sit, you know?

Carol saw your article in *Franchise Times*. We did some investigation and found out you guys were well versed in the SBA 504 loan, so we decided to call. You guys were very helpful, picked up the ball where somebody else had dropped it, and did a very good job. You all worked through it and got us to this point, so we're very appreciative of the effort of all of your staff. It really wasn't a long process. We worked with the general contractor who had built our other two stores, so it went pretty smoothly.

As I recall, the total project cost was about $1.6 million with the land, building and equipment, and I think we financed 85 percent of the total project.

Carol: Well, we appreciate everything you guys did for us. You really pulled us out of a rut here. We couldn't have opened this store without the help in the timely manner that you guys provided it. We do appreciate that a lot, and I'm glad I read the article that day.

CHAPTER SIX

The SmartChoice® Alternative

*I have no complex about wealth. I have worked hard for my money, producing
things people need. I believe that the able industrial leader who creates wealth
and employment is more worthy of historical notice than politicians and
soldiers … the meek may inherit the earth, but not the mineral rights.*
—J. PAUL GETTY

In the realm of ideas everything depends on enthusiasm.
In the real world all rests on perseverance.
—JOHANN WOLFGANG VON GOETHE

Time for some inside baseball. In this chapter, I'm going
to fill you in on a wealth of details about the SBA and
the loans it administers, in particular, the SBA 504
loan that my company, Mercantile Capital Corporation, specializes in, the one we call the SmartChoice® Commercial
Loan.

Above all else this is what I want you to know: There's an alternative to ordinary conventional bank financing. This alternative is
superior in a number of the areas that were outlined in the previous
chapter. If you're a small business owner looking to purchase commercial property for your business, the SBA 504 loan is very likely the
right one for you, and you should find a lender who specializes in it
and understands how its advantages can be applied to your situation.

Beyond that, however, if you'll humor me, let's take a look at the inner workings of this loan and the agency that has made it all possible. I want to offer you some perspective so you fully appreciate the difference a SmartChoice® Commercial Loan can mean to you and learn whether you're eligible to pursue one.

The SBA's Function

The SBA, which has been around more than half a century, is the only agency of the federal government that's committed to helping out America's small businesses and entrepreneurs with the mission of strengthening the U.S. economy. The SBA has various functions, in addition to the loan programs it promotes. It's had the historic role of helping communities to recover after disasters (even though that perhaps is a better role for FEMA), and it works to assure that a fair portion of federal contracts go to small businesses, including those owned by women and veterans who were disabled during military service, among others. The SBA also provides grants to such recipients as Small Business Development Centers (SBDCs), often on college campuses; to Women's Business Centers; and to SCORE, a mentoring group of more than 13,000 retired business leaders.

It's important to understand that the SBA does not actually lend money except for federal disaster aid. Rather, the agency is the facilitator by which the federal government merely guarantees small business loans, as you will soon see.

The Two Principal SBA Loan Programs

There are two primary SBA loans. One is called the 7(a). It was established decades ago, and has been the flagship loan program of the SBA ever since. It happens to be the program that is favored by most lenders in America. There's a reason for that: These loans have up to 75 percent guarantees on them from the government. The guaranteed portion is often sold out to investors in the secondary market, and the lenders get very nice premium fees for doing so. This increases the liquidity for these lenders, who then have new money to issue more loans. The theory is that this greases the wheels of commerce, and more capital becomes available for America's small businesses.

The SBA 7(a) loan has some downsides to it, which we'll discuss, but also plenty of upside. This is how most small business acquisitions are done in America when seller-financing isn't an option. Partner buyouts often are done with 7(a) loans. They are also frequently used for working capital and startup capital financing. They certainly have some great benefits and fill a need. Yet, the 7(a) program is not the one best-suited for a small business owner looking to buy commercial property or heavy equipment.

The other major SBA loan program is the 504, which isn't as well known, though it has been around more than thirty years. It's not as well known because it's clearly not the preference of the overall small business lending community to lead with the 504. Traditionally, ordinary lenders lead with the 7(a) when they work with small business owners.

Although the SBA has tremendous programs, the agency, like other governmental entities, is not the best promoter and educator of those very programs. It doesn't, in my opinion, do enough to help small business owners fully understand what it has to offer. I've been involved in SBA lending since the late 1990s, and I've seen the agency's promotional efforts improve markedly during that time. However, the agency still relies on its lending partners to carry the flag for its programs, and those lenders, by and large, have a clear preference for 7(a) loans in general, even for commercial property acquisitions or new property construction. For these reasons, the 504 has gone largely underused and remains underappreciated in the world of commercial real estate lending.

Comparing the SBA Loan Programs

In the fiscal year ending September 30, 2011, the SBA hit an all-time high in terms of loan production, so the programs are in fact growing. During the recent recession many ordinary commercial lenders adopted more stringent credit requirements for small business borrowers while the SBA didn't change its underwriting one bit. The SBA continued to be a very stable presence in the small business sector of our economy. More and more lenders are looking to mitigate their risk and are therefore doing more SBA loans, which is a big reason the agency's numbers were up.

The agency is finally shaking the common myth that it's a "lender of last resort." That clearly was shown not to be the case in the recent recession. The SBA has been one of the few places where small business owners could turn and actually get financing, and I think it has very bright days ahead of it. More people are learning about some of the great SBA loan programs that would otherwise be ignored or dismissed because of outdated myths that have lingered for years (more on those in the next chapter).

The 7(a) is a fully collateralized loan program, which may be why the myth persists that an SBA loan requires you to offer up your firstborn and the kitchen sink. All SBA loans require personal

SmartChoice® vs. 7(a) Comparison

The SmartChoice® Commercial Loan is more commonly known as an SBA 504 loan. When it comes to this kind of financing, which is designed specifically to finance commercial real estate and other fixed assets for small business owners, many lenders only talk about one type of SBA loan — the SBA 7(a) loan. The SBA 7(a) program is a fine program and is great for business acquisitions, partner buyouts and working capital, but it's not as good for commercial real estate as the 504. Since a commercial lender may or may not give you the full story regarding this type of financing — focusing only on the 7(a) — let's take a side-by-side look at these two loan programs:

	SmartChoice® Commercial Loans	SBA 7(a) Loans
Project Size	• $200,000 - $15,000,000	• $50,000 - $5,000,000
Uses	• Real estate • Equipment	• Real estate • Equipment • Business Acquisitions • Working Capital • Startup Financing • Partner Buyouts
Interest rate	• Choice of fixed or floating on 1st lien portion. • Below market, long-term fixed interest rate on 2nd lien portion, fixed for the entire 20 years.	• Floating rate based on Prime or LIBOR plus an interest rate spread. • Maximum rate of 2.75% over Prime.
Term/Amortization	• 20-30 years fully amortized.	• 5-25 years fully amortized, depending on the useful life of collateral.
Down Payment	• 10% of eligible project costs (borrowers can roll-in renovation, closing and soft costs). • An extra 5% is required for start-ups and/or special-use properties.	• 20-30% for start-up or business acquisition. • 10-20% for expansion.
Collateral	• Only the real estate and/or equipment being financed.	• Must be "fully collateralized," which frequently means a blanket lien filing on all assets of the business (A/R and inventory included, which may make getting a line of credit difficult) and the business owner's home.
Loan Fees	• Always lower; usually averages about 1 - 1.25% of loan amount.	• Always higher; a tiered system is in place that quickly rises to as high as 3.75% of the guaranteed loan portion (75% of the loan amount in most cases).

In most situations, a SmartChoice® Commercial loan will be the best choice for a small business owner's commercial real estate project. Just be prepared to do a little homework (this book is a great first step) and ask many to make sure you chose the right type of financing for your unique situation.

guarantees, meaning the small business owner has to sign a personal guarantee that he will repay the debt. A lot of unsophisticated small business owners and entrepreneurs think they can get around that, but it's usually not until you have had a tremendous degree of success that you can get commercial financing as a small business owner without personally guaranteeing a loan. With ordinary commercial financing, you can sometimes negotiate to have the personal guarantees taken off over time, but it doesn't work that way with an SBA loan, and from the perspective of the U.S. taxpayer, the personal guarantee is a way to hold the borrower's feet to the fire, to make sure he's committed to making the business successful and repaying the loan.

Nonetheless, just about every attorney I've ever dealt with tells small business owners to never personally guarantee anything. That clearly shows a lack of comprehension of the real world of small business finance, where, for better or worse, everything is personally guaranteed. It's just a fact of life. It's usually a red flag for me when a business owner balks at that. If you're convinced that you're going to be successful and that your business is going to do well, then having to personally guarantee a loan should be a nonissue. I should know. I've guaranteed tens of millions of dollars.

The 7(a) loan is the program that has given the SBA a bit of a black eye over the years. Again, it's the one that most lenders lead with, and the SBA oftentimes wants a second lien on the borrower's home and often requires additional life insurance, with the lender and/or the SBA as the beneficiary. Sometimes, the loan will require liens against a business' inventory, receivables, or furniture, fixtures, and equipment. That can make it much more difficult or even impossible to get a line of credit secured with that same inventory and/or receivables. It's going to complicate your life dramatically.

Another reason that lenders lead with the 7(a) is that it is pretty flexible. You can do more with the money you get from a 7(a) loan than you can with a 504. You can use a 7(a) for a business acquisition, refinancing, startup and working capital, partner buy-outs, and more.

You can also use a 7(a) loan for the purchase of commercial real estate and heavy equipment. In other words, you can use it the same way you would use a 504, but the inverse is not always true. There are certain things you can do with a 7(a) that you cannot do with a 504. The 7(a) is a much broader-based loan program. SBA 504 loans are only for hard assets, or what I call stuff that you could kick, for example, commercial real estate and heavy equipment, and also the soft costs and closing costs related to the project that you're financing.

As mentioned earlier, unlike a 7(a) loan, the SBA 504 loan is collateralized only by what is being financed, which is the commercial real estate and equipment, in most cases. There's seldom ever a claim on the borrower's house, inventory, or receivables. It's just neither necessary nor required.

Another big difference is the fact that the 7(a) will almost always have a variable or floating interest rate. In the secondary market for these loans, investors pay a hefty premium and will do so only if the loan's rate changes when there's a change in its index, usually, the Wall Street Journal Prime Rate and sometimes the LIBOR Index. That can be a problem for the small business owner because rates can change on a quarterly or even a monthly basis and most likely will in the coming years as rates rise.

For several years we've seen consistent historically low interest rates for commercial real estate financing. The historic average over the past fifty years is roughly 8.5 percent for commercial real estate. As I write this, the rate is hovering at about 5 percent. For a 7(a) loan, if the index is the prime rate, it cannot be priced at more than 2.75 over the prime rate. For example, with prime at 3.25 percent, you're at a 6 percent cap.

Unfortunately, there's nowhere to go but up from here. Interest rates have been very low for quite a while, but they'll eventually creep back to their historical average. Those rising interest rates represent a variable expense—and a painful one—to most small business owners.

I've made dozens and dozens of SBA 7(a) loans in my tenure, and early in my career we were putting loans on the streets in the 11 percent and 12 percent interest rate range. Why? Because prime was in the 9 percent and 10 percent range. The 3.25 percent prime rate as of this writing is bound to change. Rates have a tendency to revert to the mean, so a variable rate on an SBA loan will typically be in the 8.75 to 9.75 percent range. Depending on the size of the project you're financing, the rise in interest rates could add thousands of dollars more per month in debt service payments that you could otherwise be putting into your business somewhere else.

With a variable rate, you lack the certainty and stability that you get with fixed-rate financing. It's harder to plan for the future of your business, and your dreams, when you don't know for sure when your cash flow will change and by how much.

The Right Loan for You

You want to use the right tool for the job, and that holds true for financing the purchase of commercial real estate and equipment. There's not much of a difference between the 7(a) and 504 loans in terms of your down payment for commercial property, though the 7(a) in some cases requires more of a down payment. So it comes down to a matter of function: What are you financing, and how much capital do you need? Keep in mind that this isn't necessarily an either/or question. It's common to have a 504 loan for hard assets and a 7(a) loan for working capital. That way, you can capitalize on the strengths of each loan program and use them as they were designed to be used.

If your primary purpose is to acquire property or equipment, the 504 is the loan for you, for all the reasons we've discussed. The two major advantages it has over the 7(a) are its below-market, fixed interest rates and its less onerous collateral requirements.

Good for You, Good for the Economy

The SBA 504 loan is meant to encourage economic development. If small business owners can get better terms, better pricing, and an overall better loan structure, they can save more of their capital and reinvest it in their business. That typically means growth and expansion. Often that includes hiring employees to operate new equipment, handle new orders, and serve new customers.

Such activities are beneficial to our economy, and that was the reason the 504 program was conceived. That's why it exists and why the SBA tracks how many jobs are created or retained for each 504 project.

In addition to job creation/retention, the SBA also has secondary policy goals for the 504 program. These include assistance for businesses owned by minorities, women, and veterans (disabled ones especially) as well as businesses located in rural areas or inner city neighborhoods in need of revitalization. This isn't an exclusive list of SBA policy goals, but the point is that it's extraordinarily rare for a small business owner to be deemed ineligible for a 504 loan based on policy reasons.

If I can help small businesses and the SBA meet those policy goals, that's great, but at the end of the day, it comes down to the fact that we're helping American small business owners create wealth. When they create wealth, they will grow their business and hire new employees, and all of this will translate into more prosperity. If you're a small business owner who is able to buy the commercial property your business occupies, chances are you're going to be around for a while. You will, in fact, put more money into the economy, with effects lasting generations. All those positives are bound to have a stabilizing effect on our overall economy.

Are You Eligible?
Three Major Tests

There are three primary financial criteria to determine eligibility for a small business seeking a 504 loan. These criteria have been tweaked in recent years so that more small business owners are able to qualify for SBA financing.

One of them is that you cannot have a tangible business net worth greater than $15 million. That's a pretty high threshold, and few small businesses exceed that even if they're doing $20 million to $30 million a year in gross revenues. Even many large manufacturers, when they factor in the depreciation on their heavy equipment, probably won't have a tangible business net worth of greater than $15 million. In all my years of dealing with SBA financing, I don't think I've ever seen a small business turned down for a 504 loan because it exceeded this limit. Still, that's the first filter that a small business has to meet.

Nor does the second filter knock very many people out, and it too has been revised upward over the last few years: A small business applying for an SBA loan cannot have an average net income greater than $5 million over the previous two years. It used to be $2.5 million. On the heels of the Great Recession, it is unlikely that very many small business owners have an average net income of $5 million or more over the previous two years.

The third financial filter relates to the personal liquidity of each principal or guarantor, and the SBA defines a principal as someone who owns 20 percent or more of the operating company or the real estate holding company (more on this in a minute). If you are a principal or a guarantor, you cannot have personal liquidity greater than the total project cost of the proposed 504 loans. This personal liquidity test is defined as nonretirement, unencumbered liquidity.

Let me give you a hypothetical example that's similar to ones we've encountered. A physician comes to us wanting to buy a medical office condo for $300,000. This physician has been practicing for twenty-five years and has been diligent about retirement contributions. Those contributions aren't counted toward the SBA personal liquidity threshold, but he's been fairly successful, and he also has $400,000 in a stock brokerage account that's made up of stocks, bonds, and a money market account (cash). The total project cost of his medical office condo is $300,000. The SBA actually deems him ineligible because of the presumption that he has the cash on hand and could buy the property outright instead of borrowing long term. He's not about to cash out his stock brokerage account and trigger a major tax hit, so in effect, that liquidity is not quite what it seems. Despite this, he won't qualify for SBA financing. Frankly, this particular physician would probably make a really good conventional loan prospect for another commercial lender. Or, he could always go buy some large "toys" (such as a boat), as we often joke around the office when we see a situation like this.

So those are the three financial qualifiers that determine 504 eligibility. I rarely see anybody deemed ineligible based on any of those three, but they are something to consider. There used to be various criteria regarding revenue and number of employees that were applied to 7(a) loan applicants but not to 504 loan applicants. That's changed, and the remaining eligibility thresholds have risen over the years, which is a good thing, considering the effects of inflation and the growth of a typical business.

Ineligible Businesses

Certain small businesses are deemed ineligible to seek an SBA loan by their very nature. For example, nonprofits are not eligible. If you are a for-profit, non-publicly-held company, in all likelihood you are going to be eligible for a 504 loan, but if you're a nonprofit, you're generally not going to be eligible.

Nor can you be a passive holder of real estate or personal property. However, you can create a real estate holding company or what's called an eligible passive concern (EPC), which is good for general estate planning and tax purposes. I'll discuss that further later in this chapter.

Lending institutions are also ineligible to acquire SBA financing. An exception is mortgage brokers and correspondent lenders, who are deemed eligible. At Mercantile Capital Corporation, however, I would not be able to get a 504 loan for our business. I was able to invest in a 504 project separately with some friends in an engineering firm who bought an office property, but I am ineligible, using the operating business of Mercantile Capital.

You can't be a life insurance company and be eligible for 504 financing. If you're a franchised agent, however, you are usually eligible (it will depend on how your agency agreement is written, especially if you're part of a franchise like State Farm or Allstate).

List of Ineligible Businesses

Over 98% of incorporated entities in the United States are considered "small businesses" and are eligible for financing with a SmartChoice® Commercial Loan. The following is a finite list of the types of businesses that are ineligible.

- Non-profits (except sheltered workshops).
- Passive holders of real estate and/or personal property.
- Lending institutions (however, mortgage brokers and correspondent lenders are eligible).
- Life insurance companies (however, franchised agents are eligible).
- Businesses located in a foreign country or owned by aliens.*
- Businesses selling products/services through a pyramid plan.
- Illegal businesses.
- Gambling concerns.
- Businesses which restrict patronage.
- Government owned entities (excluding Native American Tribes).
- Businesses engaged in promoting religion.
- Consumer and marketing cooperatives (however, producer cooperatives are eligible).
- Businesses engaged in loan packaging.
- Businesses owned by persons of poor character.
- Businesses providing prurient sexual material.
- Businesses that have previously defaulted on a Federal loan.
- Businesses engaged in political or lobbying activities.
- Speculative businesses.

If your business doesn't fit into any of the above categories, then you're probably eligible for a SmartChoice® Commercial Loan. Now, this doesn't mean you'll qualify for a loan — you'll have to go through the Pre-Approval Process to find out for your unique business/situation — but you won't be wasting your time by doing so.

* Ownership must be comprised of 51% U.S. citizens or resident aliens (Legal Permanent Residents), but some businesses owned by Foreign Nationals or Foreign Entities may be eligible if the following three requirements are met:
  - Application must contain assurances that management is expected to continue in place indefinitely and have U.S. citizenship or verified LPR status.
  - Management must have operated the businesses for at least 1 year prior to application date.
  - The personal guaranty of management must be considered as a loan condition and if not required, the decision must be explained in the loan file.

The SBA will not finance businesses that are located in a foreign country or owned by foreigners who are not U.S. citizens or legal permanent residents with a green card. There are some exceptions to these rules, which very few lenders in the SBA industry truly understand and are partly beyond the scope of this book, but in general the SBA does not want to guarantee loans made in Canada or Mexico or elsewhere. (Note: If a simple majority of the owners of your proposed project is not made up of U.S. citizens or legal permanent residents, please contact us to learn about the various exceptions to this SBA eligibility standard.)

You can't be a business selling products or services through a pyramid scheme, and that should go without saying, since obviously you cannot be involved in an illegal business.

You cannot operate a gambling concern, so casinos will not be deemed eligible.

No business that restricts patronage can get an SBA loan. For example, golf courses are eligible for 504 financing, but not if they only allow men or people of certain races to play there.

Government-owned entities generally are not eligible, nor are businesses that engage in promoting religion. Consumer and marketing cooperatives are not deemed eligible, although producer cooperatives are eligible.

Businesses owned by persons of poor character are deemed ineligible. The SBA has a personal history form (called the 912) on which you have to check boxes asking whether you have ever committed a felony or been arrested for anything beyond a misdemeanor. If you have, you must explain. We have had instances in which the FBI had to become involved and run a check to determine how bad the offense was. A drunk-driving offense or bar scuffle back in your college days is unlikely to make you ineligible. We once had an applicant who had been a chemistry major in college, and let's just say he'd done a few things more in practicum than one would normally do in that major. He was still deemed eligible. I remember another borrower, though, who was deemed ineligible. He had a record of battery against his mother-in-law. The agency does not look kindly upon you if you beat up your mother-in-law, no matter how good you think your explanation is.

Businesses that have previously defaulted on a federal loan cannot expect to get SBA financing. Let's say a physician had a student loan, guaranteed by the government. He got all the way through school, years and years of medical education, and at some point defaulted on it. The agency will discover that, and that physician will be disqualified from pursuing an SBA loan. So, you always want to make sure you pay back your government-guaranteed debt.

Speculative businesses, however those are defined, are ineligible. I realize that it has been argued that just about every business is speculative, certainly when it's starting out, but still...

The bottom line here is that if your business didn't make this exhaustive list, you're probably going to be just fine. That's important to keep in mind. Less than 2 percent of America's businesses would be deemed ineligible based on the SBA's list, so there's no reason to feel discouraged in applying for an SBA loan. Your prospects of being eligible are really quite good.

Permissible Uses of a 504

As you know, the SBA 504 loan is mostly for fixed assets—the purchase of land and buildings—but it also can be used to make improvements to that land and those buildings. It can be used for utilities, parking lots, landscaping, grading, and street improvements, or it can be used for construction of a new facility, as well as the associated costs of that construction: impact fees, permitting fees, architecture and engineering fees, interest expense, construction contingencies, and so on. This way, the small business owner doesn't have to pay such expenses out-of-pocket on a construction project that's far from finished.

This type of financing can also be used for modernizing, renovating, and converting a facility to another use, as well as outfitting it with machinery and equipment. To be included, heavy equipment should have a useful life greater than ten years. However, small business owners have used the SmartChoice® Commercial Loan to buy office equipment, cubicles, audio/visual equipment, high-tech wiring, cabling, etc., even though they may not have quite a long-term useful life. Often, business owners pay for such things in cash or finance them over much shorter terms, but a SmartChoice® Commercial Loan specialist can include them in your commercial loan. That gives you a cash flow advantage.

You can't use a SmartChoice® Commercial Loan for operating capital or for things such as inventory purchases and paying down receivables. It used to be that you could not use it for refinances, but the Small Business Jobs and Credit Act of 2010 provided for a temporary period in which the loan could be used to refinance conventionally financed commercial mortgages. As of this writing, Congress may yet still extend this temporary measure by another year.

How the SBA 504 Program Works

The SBA 504 is structured like this: Half of it is from the lender in a first lien position. The second mortgage or trust deed portion is made by a Certified Development Company (CDC). CDCs are the SBA's representative to do 504 loans, and they ultimately take the second lien position.

The CDC finances its portion via a bond sold every month in the public markets. That means there is a period of time, perhaps a few months, between the closing of your 504 loan and the acquisition of the bond funds. Therefore the first mortgage lender either provides what's called an interim or bridge second mortgage, or another lender provides it, which is often the case in today's restrictive environment in which regulators do not want banks to be at a high loan-to-value position very long. We, at Mercantile, have worked with nearly forty banks around the country just providing this interim second mortgage portion until the SBA debenture (bond) takes us out.

The SBA has certified numerous CDCs across the country, most of them not-for-profits, and their main purpose is economic development in their communities. Some of them have functions beyond 504 loans. Some of them administer small, specialized lending programs: renovation loans to make properties environmentally friendly, perhaps small job creation grants, and similar programs. When there's a natural disaster, a lot of times CDCs will help in the administration of disaster aid monies, but in general, they're predominantly tasked with processing SBA 504 loans.

There are about 260 CDCs nationwide right now. Some CDCs do a great job, and we prefer to work with them and recommend people to them. For other CDCs, processing the 504 loans seems like an afterthought, and consequently they're not particularly good at it, and unfortunately that can harm the SBA's reputation. In Appendix

A I've listed about 150 of the very best CDCs, by state, and we at Mercantile have worked directly on 504 loans with nearly eighty of them.

So a small business owner goes to a commercial lender who wants to do a 504 loan. The lender underwrites the loan request and approves it internally. Then we send the entire loan package electronically to the CDC involved (usually the lender determines which CDC to use), and it goes through it and underwrites it objectively on its own. This does not take as long as it might seem. Most CDCs, certainly the competent ones, can usually approve a loan that's eligible within a week to ten days at the most, but it's a whole different

Interim Loan Details

There are many, many options when it comes to choosing a commercial lender for a commercial real estate project. Depending upon the project and/or current economic or regulatory environment, a significant portion of commercial lenders may balk at doing an SBA 504 loan (or SmartChoice® Commercial Loan). If or when that happens, it's possible to bring in a third-party lender (such as Mercantile Capital Corporation) to handle the interim, second lien loan and make the project doable. We've worked with more than three dozen banks and non-bank lenders to make this happen, and below are the three primary situations when it's most helpful:

1) When a lender doesn't want to provide the interim/bridge loan due to: possible regulatory pressures, legal lending limit issues, or the property type and/or credit doesn't meet that lender's loan policy guidelines.
2) When a lender doesn't want to do commercial construction and/or renovations due to risks associated with construction and/or the property type not meeting that lender's loan policy guidelines.
3) When a CDC originates a SmartChoice® loan and wants to get the authorization approved and interim lender committed in order to expedite securing a third-party (first lien) lender.

Unfortunately, a commercial lender may turn down a project because of just one thing that makes them uncomfortable. Suggesting a third-party interim lender, such as Mercantile, may make a "slightly un-doable" project "very doable" if it overcomes any of the above hurdles.

THE SMARTCHOICE® ALTERNATIVE

set of eyes, and an independent approval process, so you've basically been underwritten twice.

Then, the CDC transmits the package to the SBA's central processing center in Sacramento, California. The SBA typically gets back to them within forty-eight to seventy-two hours. If all is well, the SBA issues what's called an authorization, which the CDC then delivers to you, the borrower. The SBA 504 Loan Authorization is sort of the "playbook" on that particular 504 loan, a listing of the borrowers, guarantors, debenture amount, specific loan details, collateral, liens, and a variety of other pertinent information.

The second lien position on the 504 either has a twenty-year debenture—that would be for one that's backed by owner-occupied commercial real estate—or perhaps a ten-year debenture, for heavy machinery. The debenture is simple. It's just a bond that's sold to investors. They are getting a government guarantee—the full faith and credit of the U.S. government—on these bonds, and because of that these investors take a lower yield on the bond. The yield they're receiving is essentially the interest rate payment (plus some minor ongoing fees) that the small business owner is making. I like to think of this as bringing Wall Street to Main Street.

As I write this, for instance, the twenty-year fixed-rate debenture for the month is 4.45 percent, fixed for twenty years. That's virtually unheard of in the conventional banking community. Commercial real estate financing is getting very close to residential financing rates in fixed interest rate terms, and the reason it's so low—typically about 50 to 150 basis points below prevailing market rates for ordinary commercial property financing—is because the bond investors see these 504 loans as less risky. It is considered a very low risk investment for the investors like pension funds, college endowments, mutual funds, and the like.

I have often called the 504 debentures the least expensive financing vehicle for small business owners to own their commercial property. Nothing in the small business lending community even comes close. No banks will do a twenty-year fixed interest rate on commercial property with only 10 percent down. It just doesn't happen anywhere conventionally. It takes a 504 loan.

Every single month these bonds are sold. They range from about $200 million to about $400 million every month. There has never been a month in almost thirty years that there hasn't been a sale of 504 debentures. Even in those difficult autumn days of 2008, when a lot of people thought the sky was falling (financially speaking), the debentures continued. In fact, the December 2008 debenture amount was the largest one in 2008 in terms of funded volume.

All of this is done through this channel of the CDCs, really getting out there and trying to carry the flag for the 504. A problem is that a lot of the CDCs in the country operate as quasibureaucratic organizations. That's not a universal criticism. Many do see themselves as fulfilling this role of economic developers and really helping provide inexpensive capital to small business owners so that they can create wealth, but there are some out there, unfortunately, that are a bit slow, and many times it's because they're tasked with multiple product lines. Again, a jack of all trades tends to become a master of none, and CDCs are no different from others in this regard.

Typically, the CDC finances 40 percent of the project cost, in the junior lien position. Fifty percent comes from the private sector lender, as I've already mentioned. The difference, or 10 percent of the project cost, is the typical down payment from the small business borrower. The private sector loan will either have a fixed interest rate or a variable rate, and it will generally be at or perhaps slightly higher than ordinary conventional loan rates. Your second mortgage, or 40 percent of the loan, however, is usually considerably lower than the market rates and is fixed for the entire twenty-year term.

It doesn't always break down to the 50-40-10 structure I've outlined above, however. Occasionally, you'll see situations where it's a 60-30-10 structure, with 60 percent from the private sector lender. Or even a 50-30-20 structure when a startup *and* a special-use property are involved. These will happen from time to time; it will just depend on the particulars of that project.

Often, on what the SBA, the CDC, or perhaps a commercial appraiser deem to be a special-purpose/special-use property, you'll have a requirement by the SBA to require extra equity—that is, more of a down payment. A special-purpose property—restaurants and hotels, a marina, perhaps a day care—might require an additional 5 percent equity contribution.

Also, businesses that are considered startups might require more down payment contributions as well. If you are a franchise restaurateur, opening a second location, however, it might be considered a continuation of your existing business, per SBA guidelines. Since you're already in the industry, it won't be considered a startup, but if it is a true startup, the SBA will probably require at least 15 percent down—the normal 10 percent, plus the 5 percent extra for the special-purpose project—and then, in the case of some "large" startups, an additional 5 percent. So in those cases, even under the 504 structure, you'll be getting 80 percent loan-to-cost financing. In these situations, however, an ordinary conventional lender (assuming such a company would even lend) would most likely require 30 percent to 35 percent as a down payment.

The huge advantage of having a low down payment is clear: You have more cash on hand to do with what you want. If you can come to the table with half the down payment, half the capital requirement that the conventional lender wants from you, you can turn around and use your equity savings for other purposes. You'll have more operating capital to run your business or even better your business.

So in the instance of special-purpose property financing, at an 85 percent loan-to-cost financing, you still are doing far better than you would with conventional financing, in which you would face 60 percent to 70 percent loan-to-value financing. It's a dramatic difference, and it highlights a recurring theme of this book: capital utilization, or how can you stretch your dollars as far as possible.

With the SmartChoice® Commercial loan, you have two separate loans, so in effect you get a blended interest rate. We simply proportionalize the interest rates of the first mortgage and the second mortgage. If you have a typical 50-40-10 structure, the first mortgage piece is going to be 56 percent of your total loan payment, while your second mortgage piece will be 44 percent. We simply take whatever your interest rate is on the first mortgage (for example, 5.5 percent on 56 percent of the project cost) and the interest rate on the second mortgage (perhaps 4.45 percent on 44 percent of the project cost), and we run a calculation to come up with your below-market, blended interest rate (in this case, it would be 5.04 percent).

That's the proper way to look at this. You cannot merely compare the interest rate on the first mortgage under a 504 Loan to the rate on an ordinary commercial loan. That doesn't give you an accurate picture. The interest payments that you're going to report on your tax returns are in fact the interest payments on both the first and the second, and therefore, you should consider your rate as a blend of the two.

That's why, in many respects, comparing an ordinary commercial loan to the SmartChoice® Commercial Loan is really an apples to oranges comparison. The interest rate with the SmartChoice® loan will almost always be considerably lower. In many cases, the Smart-Choice® loan will also have a longer amortization and a longer fixed-

rate period, plus it won't have required as much of a down payment as an ordinary conventional loan. As you can see, there are a lot of differences.

To make it easier and simpler to compare different types of commercial loans, we developed a smartphone app called the SmartChoice® Commercial Loan Calculator. It's available for both iOS (iPhone/iPad) and Android operating systems, and it answers the most frequently asked questions we get from small business owners: What will my down payment be? How much will my monthly payments be? What are the current interest rates? What are my loan options? Our Smart-Choice® App will give you

helpful loan comparisons, allow you to save and e-mail calculation results for future reference, and give you access to even more commercial financing resources. Oh, and it's absolutely free. Just search for "smartchoice calculator" in the iTunes store or Google Play, or go to www.504Experts.com for more information and to download the app.

Avoiding Hassles

A criticism that people have of SBA lending is that the process takes far too long, but that's a myth. Any delay most likely would be caused by the commercial lender that the borrower has chosen rather than the process itself, or the agency. It's safe to say that these loans can be closed, start to finish, in forty-five days or less. Our record is twenty-six days from the moment I first spoke to the client on the telephone to the time we got him to the closing table. The stars have to align perfectly for that to happen, but my point is that you should not worry about the process taking too long. In most cases, commercial real estate is financed; very little of it is paid for in cash. Therefore, most commercial real estate contracts are written for the property to close within 60 to 120 days. The contracts do often have contingencies for financing concerns, environmental studies, and so on, but those are very normal. There is more than enough time for a competent lender to process a 504 loan.

Obviously, time does mean money to a business, so my company works as fast as it can. At times it can feel, however, that we hurry up and wait. By that I mean we do our best to expedite the financing process, but completing the paperwork might not be the highest priority on a given day for our small business clients. Being a small business owner myself, I understand that many days seem to get swallowed up by a myriad of concerns. Collecting personal tax returns from three years ago might not be the first thing you tackle when you start your day. Our clients will eventually get it all together and get it done, but we (or any other lender) can't proceed until we get all that information. We also have a number of third parties involved in the lending process, and so, often we're waiting for the commercial appraiser to get the appraisal back; we're waiting for an environmental firm to give us our environmental report—you don't want to buy a property that's contaminated, or you'll be assuming that liability—or we're waiting for the surveyor. Often, we're waiting for the title company agent to send the title insurance over. Many things come into play here. There are a lot of moving parts. I do believe that we're the fastest folks around in the commercial lending arena, yet we also depend on others, and sometimes they slow everyone else down.

Again, your best strategy for a trouble-free experience is to work with a specialist and to take steps to become preapproved before you decide on the commercial property you want to buy. You don't want to be practice for somebody who does only one or two of these loans a year. That's why it's good to directly ask, "How many of these loans have you done, and can you give me the names of former clients who can talk with me about their experience with you?"

Our goal at Mercantile is to streamline the lending process as much as possible to avoid the hassles. We believe that the commercial financing experience doesn't have to be one of teeth gnashing, which is the perception that's out there for many people, and I think if you spoke to most of our clients, they'd agree that we make what appears to be an arduous process, a very streamlined one, maybe even enjoyable, if that's a word that can actually be in a sentence about commercial real estate financing.

Creative Financing Through Holding Companies

In pursuing an SBA504 loan, there are even more advantageous steps you can take that many people are not aware of, but which the program allows.

For example, a business owner can either purchase and hold title to the building personally; hold title in the name of the business; or do what most of our clients do and set up a real estate holding company or what's otherwise called an eligible passive concern (EPC). Most of them do that because it makes more sense, for long-term planning purposes, to separate their operating company from the real estate. In this structure, the holding company takes title to the commercial property, and in this case, the SBA does not view the business as a passive holder of that real estate, which would otherwise make it ineligible for a 504 loan.

A master lease ties the property back to the operating company within this structure. If you are buying more space than you currently need, you then could sublet that space to help defray the cost of your commercial mortgage, a tactic I often suggest and one that is also permissible by the SBA. (Note: When utilizing this tactic, a master lease is typically drafted showing 100 percent occupancy of the space by the operating company. Per SBA guidelines, commercial property must be at least 51 percent owner-occupied to qualify for SBA financing.)

Like most small business owners, you are either going to sell the business or shut it down someday. That's typically the way you'll "exit" the operating company's business. The EPC is a mechanism through which that can happen smoothly: You will continue to own the asset but now become a landlord to someone else other than just to yourself. You can be a landlord to whoever bought your business, perhaps, or the landlord to your children if you pass the business on to them. The bottom line is, however, that this is one way to create additional wealth, and this very mechanism is how that can be accomplished. It's completely acceptable to the SBA, and it's done all the time.

Another advantageous thing that a lot of people (even seasoned SBA lenders) don't realize is that two or more small businesses can attain a SmartChoice® Commercial Loan if they come together to form an EPC. Let me give you an example. Say you have a 5,000-square-foot office building that a small specialty architectural firm would love to own, but that's a little too much space for the firm. However, it works regularly with an engineering firm that is also looking to own its own space, but 5,000 square feet would be too big for that firm too. If they were to come together, 2,500 square feet for each for them would be perfect. This is an ideally located building for both parties, and they both like what it looks like and the condition it's in. These two firms could come together and form an EPC, through which they would own the building together, with one partner meeting the simple majority (51 percent) owner-occupancy requirement of the SBA. As a lender, we would take a look at the financials from each business, effectively combining them into one, and that's how we would underwrite their loan for approval purposes.

Under an EPC structure, you will still maintain the many tax benefits of ownership as well. Let's say your operating company makes a $10,000 monthly rent payment to your EPC. As the owner of your EPC, you're taking noncash expenses such as depreciation and amortization against that monthly income. You're also writing off your interest expense from your loans. Remember: under a 504 loan structure, this interest expense includes a first lien loan and a second lien loan, and so, while you're taking in $10,000 a month, you in effect may end up legitimately reducing what you ultimately are taxed on, perhaps reducing it to $7,000 a month or even less. That's a benefit of doing this wealth enhancement strategy under this EPC structure.

Of course, all parties would need to talk to their accountants and lawyers about the arrangement, but this can be a very wise move. Doing an EPC structure can also minimize liability concerns and help with long-term estate planning. Ownership options can be tailored to meet small business owners' needs. This gives the small business owner flexibility to do what is best suited for him and his company.

It Comes Down to This

SmartChoice® Commercial Loans (aka SBA 504 loans) are the least expensive financing available for most small business owners. Very few banks and private lenders can match the rates and terms that are available on a SmartChoice® Commercial Loan.

Even if a traditional or ordinary lender somehow offers a slightly lower interest rate, you have to consider the substantial difference in down payments. To me, that is the biggest buying variable to look at here. Because you don't have to put so much down, you can invest that money into your business or somewhere else, and even at a very conservative investment rate (should you put it into some savings-type account), you're going to come out well ahead.

That's just one of many considerations to make when you buy commercial property. The amount of your monthly payment is another major one, which the length of your amortization can affect more than anything. Other important considerations, as we have seen, are the collateral that you have to pledge, the favorable interest rates, and the fact that you can roll in the financing costs.

Put them together, and it's obvious that with a SmartChoice® Commercial Loan, you're going to get the least expensive financing that's out there. You can preserve your capital to better grow your business and create wealth for yourself for many years to come. As our motto says, we are "Fulfilling Dreams with Smarter Financing."

CLIENT SPOTLIGHT

SARAH BRAZIER, LIBERTY ACADEMY
LIBERTY CITY, FLORIDA

Sarah Brazier recently completed construction of and opened Liberty Academy, a new day-care facility serving Liberty City in the Miami, Florida, area. Her mission is to provide first-class services to this historically underserved community.

How did you get involved in all this? What made you decide to do this?

I had a long career in telecommunications and data communications, and I had a chance to take the five-plus-five offer and do early retirement. It was great because I had a daughter who was just turning five years old and starting kindergarten, and my husband wanted to go ahead and do this, so it was a great opportunity. I took the offer, moved down here, and was toying around with what kind of business I wanted to start because I knew I wanted to start my own business.

We moved from Georgia, and here in South Florida, it seems like everybody's got their own business—I mean, everything under the sun. So, I talked to several different people and then tried a couple of different things which I thought I might be passionate about. By the time I really got into it, I decided that I just wasn't passionate about it. I came into [child care] having always loved children. I did a lot of volunteering with various orphanages and things like that throughout Maryland, where I was from. I have a friend who owned a couple of day cares, and I was talking to her about it.

When I saw the kids, I was smitten. I said, "This is it." I felt it in my spirit.

I had to go through all of the training and the preparation and the credentialing that's all required, and with good reason, to work in this field.

Tell me about your facility.

Actually, it was an old, dilapidated, really wrecked house where various vagrants were living on almost an acre of beautiful property. It was full of mattresses and iguanas and, I mean, everything under the sun. Once we decided to do the venture, we said we wanted to own our own building. We also knew we wanted to be in an underserved community. That's another thing I'm pretty passionate about, and always have been. This was obviously an underserved community. We looked at the property and fell in love with it. There were trees in the back for the playground area, and I said, "This is it," even though I knew it would be quite an adventure to get the property and build the facility.

Well, it's a good location too, because there's an apartment complex right here.

Right behind us. Now, when we bought the property, that was a tenacre trailer park, and we didn't know that they were going turn it into an apartment complex until we started the zoning process. They said, "Oh yeah, right there. That's going be apartments," and we said, "Wow!" We didn't know how long it would take to build, but they were finished before our project was. A brand-new, beautiful, twenty-unit apartment complex, right on our back doorstep.

You took this facility from a dilapidated building to what it is today. How many square feet is it?
It's about 4,600 square feet, and it's beautiful, raised ceilings. We ended up tearing down the entire old building. We should have just torn it down from the get-go and started new. We had no idea what it took to completely renovate something. We definitely learned a lot throughout the whole process. We could have mowed it down and started fresh, and it probably would have been finished a lot quicker. We really just kept the foundation and the original front of the building, and we kept some of the foundation walls. That was it. Everything else is brand new. It's invigorating. The neighbors still come up and say, "Oh, your building is so beautiful. It's just done so much for the community."

We're now up to about a three dozen clients who are very similar to you in that they've taken some structure, be it a house or another commercial property, and transformed it into a beautiful and useful office building or day care or what have you. It's really very impressive. You're already at capacity, right?
Yes. We have eighty children enrolled, but we plan on increasing our enrollment to about a hundred, and that's just the day program. We operate twenty-four hours a day,

and we could potentially add another sixty with our night program, but realistically we're thinking that thirty children overnight would be good.

What kind of staffing issues does a twenty-four-hour operation pose for you?
Well, the fortunate thing about being in an underserved community is you have people who are very eager to work, even parttime hours. The unfortunate part is they usually have a full-time job *plus* a part-time job, but we've had an abundance of people coming and applying and inquiring about positions.

People are always going to be an issue. I managed for years in the technology field, and 80 percent of the job was just dealing with people issues. So, I was prepared for this, even though it's a different industry and there are different issues.

You said you really wanted to go and do your own thing. Where does that come from? Were your parents small business people?
Well, actually, my mother was the first black supervisor at Londontown Manufacturing. They used to make raincoats. She didn't go to college. My dad worked at Bethlehem Steel, never went to college. I had a blue-collar upbringing, but my mom bought a house when I was like six or seven in an area that was transitional. We were floored—we had a yard; we had a house. Therefore, we also went to schools that were very good, and so it really benefited us. This was outside Baltimore.

I've had various people in my family who have been entrepreneurial, but it's just something that I knew I always
wanted to do. When you work in a big corporation for so
many years, you dream of one day doing your own thing,
having a vision, doing it. It's great to do something that
you're passionate about versus something that you do just
to make money. I have a passion for kids. Of course, it
comes with all those little runny noses, but it's all worth it.

Your husband is still in the big corporate setting, isn't he?
Yeah, he works for the Small Business Administration, but
he's also passionate about this [venture]. He's very, very
supportive, as you know. He actually spends as much time
as he can here. I can't tell you how many times he comes
home at midnight because he'll go to work, and then he'll
come here and load software or whatever needs to be done.
Mopping floors—we do it all. My daughter loves it here.
I didn't know how much she would enjoy it at first. She
actually provides support for the teachers. She'll go from
teacher to teacher to see what needs to be done. She'll read a
story to the two-year-olds; she'll help three-year-olds lay out
mats. She'll be the "runner" and make copies. It's amazing. I
thought she'd just want to play with the other kids, but she
doesn't. She really tends to do more managing. It will all be
hers one day.

Besides twenty-four hour day-care services, what else
differentiates your business?
Our brochure says, "Best Quality Childcare" on it. That's
truly what we strive to provide. Being an underserved

community, there aren't many "quality" facilities for parents to choose from. When [local] people come here for the first time, they're floored. It's new; it's clean; they actually see learning materials that are available to the children. They see the uniforms and see that everything's neat and clean. You also don't want them to think this is just a babysitting service, and they love the video surveillance cameras. We've got the surveillance of classrooms available. We're having the software developed so that they can go right to our website, point, click, put in their user ID, and they can observe their child's classroom.

And then we have the twenty-four hour service for obvious reasons. A lot of these folks work bizarre hours—one to nine at night. Now they have coverage and don't have to worry about it. Most day cares close at 6 or 7 p.m., or, if they *are* open late, they're not as nice about it as the parents would like them to be.

And who designed the brochure?
Actually, my daughter did, and she's quite proud of it. So, you see [the brochure] first, and how we and the facility look. Then there's the curriculum. We make sure [the parents] understand that we're not just a babysitting facility where children sit and watch TV or just play without any structure. We clearly have a structure. We also focus on the creative curriculum, a curriculum called Beyond Centers & Circle Time. It sort of focuses on the Montessori model, where you see where the child is going developmentally, and it gives you some direction in terms of their early literacy

and things like that. It's definitely not a "ditto sheet" curriculum, where the kids are constantly just marking and marking. It's much more creative learning.

What is your competition around here?
Well, the nearest day care, believe it or not, is the YMCA right around the corner, and there are several smaller day cares, but what we offer—the curriculum, the cleanliness, the learning materials, the twenty-four-hour service, the park-like playground—all of these are tremendous selling points. A lot of child care providers' goal is to have as many children enrolled at the facility as possible. We take a different approach. Yeah, we could have made [our facility] twice as big on the same property. Would we have accomplished what we wanted to do? No. We would have given up a lot, and we wouldn't have the open space that we have.

How do you market the business?
This is something that I would have never believed, but the woman who taught me, Dr. Linda Siegel—she was also on Governor Jeb Bush's Early Childhood Coalition—said, "You can spend a lot of money on advertising in newspapers, but day-care centers make it by word of mouth and drive-bys." So let me tell you, I had done dozens of investigations into direct mailers because, as you know, we did the early enrollment. Since we had the "privilege" of being in construction for so long, our sign was up for a *long* time.

Well, that's advertising, right?
Yes, and we had about sixty early enrollments before we even opened. Before we knew it, we were close to maxed

out, so that was pretty fabulous. I didn't do the targeted marketing, but I did investigate it and got pricing. They did a list for me for all households within a three-mile radius. That would have cost me about $1,000. It turned out that I never had to spend the money, never had to pay to advertise anywhere. So, it's been pretty amazing because she was absolutely right.

Tell me about owning this property instead of leasing it.
We never even considered leasing property for obvious reasons: appreciation, the stability of knowing how much money you owe and when, etc. I know that some people do the leasing thing and do it very successfully, but the strip-mall/shopping-center day care has never appealed to me for my child.

How did you decide on us?
I got in touch with a loan officer at Florida First Capital [Finance Corporation] (FFCFC) a (certified development company), and he said, "Okay, let me find a banker. I don't think it'll be a problem. You've got good credit." He came back and told me that I should get in contact with you at Mercantile Capital Corporation. [Your people] made it clear that they bought into our model and would take us exactly where we wanted to go and encouraged us with our plan for expansion in the future.

What is your fondest memory of your business career thus far?

We used to drive by this place when it was ratty, and I would envision a nice, pretty building, and I would envision children coming in. I would envision the teachers, and after we had been in business for, I don't know, three weeks or a month or something, there it was. I saw my dream. It was absolutely that, and that was the tops. I saw it in the cameras. I'd just look at each classroom; I'd look at the playground, and they were doing it. The children were laughing and they were learning, and that was it. That was the dream.

What's your biggest obstacle that you've faced so far in business?

I would say it had to be dealing with the construction of this building, because when you work in a large corporation, you have a multimillion-dollar company behind you, so people pay attention to you.

I mean, you say something, and they do it. When you're working with customers, everybody's professional. People come through. They say they're going to do it, and they do it. Everybody wants to be at their very, very best. Here, it was a challenge because I was dealing with people who were not as professional as I was used to. I was dealing with people who were not as committed to "shining," so it was a real eye opener. I mean, they just didn't care. It was very different. The building department was even a lot more challenging than some of the other companies I had to deal with back in the day when I was working with proposals and bids. It was just different.

What's the biggest lesson you've learned so far, in this or your previous career?

It really does matter to do what you're passionate about. It really does matter, because, from the time we bought this place until the time we opened, it was about three years. When I started the project, if anybody had said it was going to be three years, I would have said, "NEXT! Let's do something else, because I don't want to wait three years." But then you're in it, and you're trying to make it happen, and you're passionate about it. When I open the doors, I'm still passionate about it, and all I can say is, "Wow." You know, I'm not even mad [about the delays]. I'm not ready to sell it. I'm really still passionate about it, so that, to me, was the key thing. I was comparing this to my biggest highlight when I worked in telecom, which was when we won a $1.2 billion contract with one of the government agencies. I won't mention who, but it took us five years to win that thing, and I just thought that was the pinnacle of everything, and, "Wow, we did it!" But now I realize that this is even more significant to me than that—than a $1.2 billion contract.

It's apparent that the community's really gotten behind what you're doing here. This is really what our type of financing is all about.

I remember Geof saying, "Sarah, this is what we're here for—to make this stuff happen for you that will provide a boost for the neighborhood and surrounding area."

It's gratifying because a lot of the things that we do—obviously, the financing we do—help to create jobs, provide economic stimulation. It's just amazing when we get to see firsthand how one of our clients has been able to make such a significant impact with the business that we've helped finance.

My loan officer used to get so excited when I would send him before-and-after pictures. Then you or Geof would send me a note and say, "Oh, it looks good!" And I could tell that you guys were really into it. You bought into it, and it just really meant a lot.

◇◇◇

CHAPTER SEVEN

Exploding the Myths

An ounce of action is worth a ton of theory.
—RALPH WALDO EMERSON

The Constitution only gives people the right to pursue happiness.
You have to catch it yourself.
—BENJAMIN FRANKLIN

W hen we don't understand something or particularly like it, it's human nature to blame that thing. It's awfully easy to throw a faceless government agency like the SBA under the bus, and that happens quite regularly.

Commercial lenders who aren't very skilled at small business lending fall back on this technique with great frequency. I understand the reason they do it, but I don't think it's terribly ethical, and it's time for it to stop.

Like urban legends, these things can take on a life of their own. Small business owners are busy. They don't have time to research such matters for themselves, and they tend to rely on their bankers as trusted advisors in positions of authority even when what they're saying is far from the truth.

I don't want to sound like a conspiracy theorist here, but a lot of bankers don't like the SBA 504 program because of what they perceive as added complexity and reduced compensation to themselves. They put out a lot of misinformation and perpetuate these myths. It's often damaging to the small business owner.

In this chapter, I will correct that misinformation. I've covered some of it in the preceding chapters, but there's much more to tell. For now, it's time to banish the top ten myths:

- Myth #1: SBA takes too long.
- Myth #2: SBA loans have too much paperwork.
- Myth #3: SBA loans are only for the worst borrowers or for startups.
- Myth #4: SBA loans have too many fees.
- Myth #5: SBA loan interest rates are higher than conventional lending's rates.
- Myth #6: SBA loans require a lien on your home.
- Myth #7: Business owners can only get one SBA loan because there's a $2 million cap.
- Myth #8: Because SBA loans are a government program, all SBA lenders are the same.
- Myth #9: Getting an SBA loan is like stealing from the poor, and only needy, minority-run-business owners should apply for them.
- Myth #10: There is a $6 million revenue limit that is imposed by lenders in deciding who gets loans.

Myth #1: SBA financing takes too long: This is a relic of the past. Perhaps it was once a fact, more than a decade ago at the SBA, but as I often tell people, if your SBA loan is taking longer than a conventional loan, you probably have the wrong lender, perhaps a novice. It shouldn't be the agency that gets the blame.

During the last fifteen years that I've been in small business lending, I've seen the agency make great strides to reduce paperwork and to expedite approvals. A lot of the CDCs we work with take our documentation electronically, which saves the time that you would otherwise have to spend in sending documents through the mail or other delivery service. They then submit materials electronically through the centralized processing center in Sacramento. The SBA has been coming through with approvals in forty-eight to seventy-two hours in most cases, weeks faster than it used to take. Sluggishness is just not the case anymore.

Fortunately, technology has helped us dramatically here, as well as the agency's attitude and the streamlining of government in general. You may hear horror stories that it takes six months to get an SBA loan done, but it frankly is not the case anymore. If it happens occasionally, there is likely an explanation. Perhaps an environmental contamination on the property required a study and cleanup. Those circumstances certainly could delay a closing, but it happens rarely with a "normal" closing. Sixty to ninety days is a very reasonable and achievable time frame for a loan to close, the same time frame as is common on the conventional commercial loan side.

Myth #2: SBA loans involve too much paperwork: Again, this is an impression from the past. In general, the documentation that the borrower needs to provide to the lender isn't any more than that required for most conventional loans. You have to sign three or four additional pages, and you may have to fill out your name and address a few extra times on the SBA's application materials, but that's about it.

We're talking about ten to fifteen minutes more effort here. In the grand scheme of things, that's pretty reasonable given all the benefits that come with this type of financing. If you run a sophisticated business with numerous entities and file various tax returns and financial statements, the paperwork can seem extensive, but in this day and age, with banking regulations as they are, any commercial loan from a bank or a credit union is going to require all that documentation as well. Once there was a great gulf between what was required for an ordinary commercial loan and what was required for an SBA loan, but they are virtually the same now.

Myth #3: SBA loans are only for the worst borrowers or for startups: Some commercial lenders have long looked down their noses at SBA lending, considering it a last resort, and that's unfortunate. They think of the SBA's 7(a) and 504 loans as interchangeable, but as I've already shown you, they're not. As we have discussed, these loans serve different purposes and operate separately under the SBA's umbrella.

I can understand why an ordinary commercial lender would disparage the SBA. In the early days, conventional loans often would have a lower interest rate and perhaps be less burdensome in terms of collateral and documentation required, but the SBA has shown that it is an enduring source of funding for the small business community, a fact quite evident since we have come through the Great Recession. It has been there for small business owners when lots of other sources evaporated.

The perception that interest rates are much higher with 7(a) loans comes and goes with time. It depends on the prime rate at any given time. In several years, when the prime rises and all lending rates go up, SBA loans (or at least those in the 7(a) program) could be back to double digit interest rates again, and I imagine ordinary commercial lenders might again spew forth such misinformation that the SBA is only for bottom-of-the-barrel borrowers.

Along with that perception is the fact that bankers don't particularly like to finance startups. Startup financing and working-capital financing is available from 7(a) lenders, and we do some startups at Mercantile with 504 loans, but most are actually franchise concepts, not what I would term traditional startups. Still, ordinary commercial lenders have long held the notion that SBA lending is somehow beneath them.

We take pride in the fact that well over 80 percent of our clients could have gotten ordinary commercial financing—they weren't startups and were very bankable—but instead they *chose* to get a 504 loan for all of the reasons we have discussed. It was the *smart* decision, not their only option.

Myth #4: SBA loans have too many fees: This myth is like a lot of the others, coming from the 7(a) side, which tends to get a little more media attention than the 504, but 7(a)s actually have reasonable fees. They have a tiered fee structure, and it starts at 2 percent of the loan amount and goes up as the loan amount goes up, as high as 3.75 percent. So, if you just superficially look at SBA loans, it could be easy to conclude that they all have high fees. The 504 loan has some fees involved with the debenture amount, but they're financed into that debenture, the second mortgage piece, and aren't really "felt" by borrowers. There will be an origination fee on the first mortgage of a 504 project because that piece is a conventional loan, and that's a common fee in the commercial loan marketplace, anywhere from half a percent of the amount financed to perhaps two percentage points. It will depend on the marketplace and on the credit quality of the applicant. For the second mortgage piece, the fees work out to about a point and a half, maybe two points, and again, those fees are included (or financed) into the 504 loan amount, unlike most ordinary commercial loans where the fees are added to the down payment at the closing table.

On a 504 loan, it may be a fair criticism that perhaps the fees are half a percentage point higher (fifty basis points higher) than what you could have with an ordinary commercial loan, but it's probably best to think of that as the cost of getting a far superior loan product. After all, you only have to put half to a third as much money down, and it's the least expensive financing vehicle in the marketplace. With below-market interest rates fixed for twenty years, that's money well spent.

Myth #5: SBA loan interest rates are higher than conventional lending's rates: This is definitely a perception from the SBA 7(a) loan program. Those rates are based on an index, plus a spread above that index to create the total interest rate. For 7(a) loans, the traditional index is the prime rate, and the maximum that an SBA 7(a) lender can charge is prime plus 2.75 percent. As I write this, the prime rate is 3.25, which puts you at 6 percent. That's a reasonably attractive rate, slightly higher perhaps than the market rate, but certainly terrific by historical measures.

However, because the vast majority of SBA 7(a) loans are floating rate loans, as the prime index moves up, as it inevitably will, that interest rate will move up. Short-term rates such as the prime rate have been artificially low compared to market rates and are poised to go back to their historical average along with other indexes (such as ten-year Treasury yields), rising back from 5.25 percent to 6.25 percent. Most SBA 7(a) lenders are currently adding that 2.75

percent spread. They sometimes charge less—prime plus one, or plus a half, or plus two—but they often add the maximum spread these days, especially in this low interest rate environment. This is where this notion that SBA loans are more expensive than ordinary commercial loans originated. It certainly is not the case with 504 loans. The 504 loans, as we have seen, are at below-market, fixed interest rates for the second mortgage piece. The first mortgage piece is at the prevailing market interest rates. So when you blend those rates, you will be at a below-market interest rate.

Myth #6: SBA loans require a lien on your home: Once again, this impression results from the 7(a) side of SBA lending. As you now know, the 7(a) is a fully collateralized government loan program. A lot of small business owners obviously have an issue with that. They don't like to have to pledge their personal property as collateral. They don't want to mix "personal business" with "business business," but it's a fact of life for those loans and difficult to get around. You can think of it as holding borrowers accountable to the U.S. taxpayers. They're less likely to walk away from their loan, default and go into foreclosure if they also risk losing their personal property. For the lender, it makes sense from a risk management standpoint to ask for this "protection" collateral.

This is not the case, however, in an SBA 504 loan. As I've said before, the SBA 504 loan uses the underlying asset(s) as collateral for the loan. Only in very rare cases does a CDC ask the borrower to pledge additional collateral. In fact, I think I've only seen that happen a half-dozen times in my entire career, and I've only seen personal property such as a home pledged as additional collateral for a 504 loan once or twice.

Myth #7: Business owners can only get one SBA loan because there's a $2 million cap: It used to be that there was a $2 million cap on the SBA guaranteed portion, but it's been raised to a $5 million cap. That was changed as part of the U.S. Jobs and Credit Act of 2010, in which the agency upwardly revised these thresholds. Because this is clearly an advantageous program for small business owners in America, it has to have a limit. Without a cap, it could not be sustained forever for everybody. So this is an acceptable limit that we can all live with for now.

In the 7(a) program, you can get a $5 million total loan with the government guarantee. However, in the 504 program, that $5 million cap only applies to the second mortgage/trust deed piece. On the first mortgage piece, you could go up to about $6.5 million, maybe even $7.5 million or more. That means you might be able to use the 504 to finance a $12 million total project, compared with a maximum of $5 million with a 7(a) loan.

If the project is considered "green," the SBA 504 second mortgage/trust deed can be up to $5.5 million, and a lot of people even in the small-business lending industry don't realize that. A green project would be one that reduces an existing business's energy consumption by at least 10 percent; one that uses a building design that reduces use of fossil fuels, other nonrenewable resources, or that minimizes the impact on the environment; or one that makes use of renewable energy sources.

If all of your projects qualify as green, there is no total cap whatsoever. You can undertake as many of those projects as you want with a $5.5 million debenture for each on the second mortgage/trust deed part. That's a huge opportunity, and as more and more people learn about this, I believe you'll see this option used heavily, such as in the hospitality (hotel) space. As I mentioned earlier, a lot of limited-service hotels are financed with SBA 504 loans—Comfort Inns, Hampton Inns, Residence Inns, Fairfield Inn & Suites, Holiday Inn Express, Best Westerns, Super 8s, etc.—and once this provision becomes more widely known, I predict lots of hotel owners and others who can see this opportunity are going to "go green" and capitalize on this provision.

Myth #8: Because SBA loans are a government program, all SBA lenders are the same: Now that you've gotten this far in the book, I would hope you see that is clearly *not* the case. As in a lot of arenas of life, there is a great difference in the competencies of the people you deal with. That's why I have been emphasizing that you want to deal with a specialist, not a generalist. These loans require a fair amount of skill and specialized knowledge. I could fill volumes with the minutiae involved in effectively handling these loans, but that would only destroy more trees and make for a very dull tome. By dealing with people with proven daily success in a specialty, you get the advantage of years of their experience and knowledge. For example, if you wanted a line of credit, you'd probably go to somebody who finances lines of credit regularly. A specialist has mastered your specific need; deal with any others at your peril.

Myth #9: Getting an SBA loan is like stealing from the poor, and only needy, minority business owners should apply for them: This myth tends to be more prevalent in favorable economic times. In more challenging times, such as now, it doesn't come up as much. You might take this view if you think the government shouldn't have a role in anything but protecting our borders. I think that's a somewhat naïve viewpoint. There are many great government programs, but very few are as beneficial, both to the recipient and to the U.S. taxpayer, as SBA programs (the 504, especially). That's because a lot of government programs are not structured as public-private partnerships that benefit all parties, as is the case with SBA loans.

The fees that the borrowers and lenders pay are, in effect, put into a pool to cover any losses in the program, preventing taxpayers from having to ever "take it on the chin." Both the 504 and the 7(a) loan programs were classified as zero-subsidy or budget-neutral programs until the Great Recession/Panic hit and took its toll there.

Think about this: Are you going to reject your Social Security check when you reach your retirement age? No doubt you feel that's money you paid into the system, that you earned and have a right to collect. Likewise, if you're an eligible small business owner, then you've earned the right to partake of these programs. This isn't the "government help" that some people decry. Rather, this is a government program that is delivered by the private sector and that is paid for by the small business owners who receive the loans and the private-sector lenders who make them. To reject these loan programs because of some myth would be unwise and, more than likely, costly to you.

Myth #10: A $6 million revenue limit is imposed by lenders in deciding who gets loans: It's true that 7(a) loans used to have various revenue caps and a number-of-employees cap, but that's never been the case for SBA 504 loans. For example, a restaurateur who had gross revenues of more than $6 million a year was ineligible for SBA 7(a) financing. While that cap was recently eliminated, it has never applied to 504 loans. We have clients who have qualified for SBA 504 financing with more than $100 million in gross revenues and hundreds of employees. Some might think these aren't very "small" businesses, but I can assure you that plenty of restaurateurs, contractors, and manufacturers are properly considered "small" even though they have more than fifty employees.

Those who are trying to compete against this clearly superior product will sometimes throw out such misinformation as I have covered here. Perhaps some of it was once factual, but those people risk embarrassing themselves, in my opinion, by continuing to perpetuate these outdated myths. You're better off avoiding someone when they bring up one of these myths. Consider it an insight into their lack of up-to-the-minute expertise on these fine lending programs.

◇◇

CLIENT SPOTLIGHT

MADDIE SUTPHIN, CONSUMER CONNECTIONS INC.
APOPKA, FLORIDA

Maddie Sutphin, founder and owner of Consumer Connections Inc., had a project very near and dear to us. We had the privilege of working through several tough issues with the purchase and build-out of her new facility in Apopka, Florida.

How did you get started in market research?

I started at NFO (one of the top five companies in this industry) doing consumer research, mostly surveys over the phone. Then I went to another company that did automotive research, ended up meeting a friend of mine in London at a conference, and he hired me and took me down to South Florida where I worked in syndicated research. From there I went back to automotive, got laid off, and came back down to Florida and started a company out at Universal Studios. I went out on my own in 1997 and started working from my home as a consultant. In 2001 I opened up my little place across the street [from my new location].

What made you want to go into business for yourself?

I decided that nobody was going to control my life again. In the past, I've been put in situations where I felt my ethics were questioned, and I knew there had to be a better way. Here, I can do things my way and make sure that my employees don't have to face the same problems that I did early on.

What services do you offer?

We primarily do data collection. Our facility is unique in that we have our own fragrance rooms. There are only four other companies out there, outside of "fragrance palaces" that have market research testing facilities with fragrance rooms in them. I also do laundry testing, another unique element of our company. Like I said, we primarily do data collection, but we also do full-service work, which includes more in-depth analysis. Primarily I like to keep with the data collection. That's what I know, that's what I can control, and that's the fun part of it.

How have you managed the growth?

I'm taking it one step at a time, even though I have grown quite rapidly over the last four years. I'm trying to keep a balance between the amount of work and the number of employees and their level of experience with market research. If there's a job that we can't handle, I don't take the work. I'm up front with my clients, and if there's something I can't do or I feel my team is not ready to do, I have no problem recommending other clients or suppliers to use.

I have a great core group of people who have helped me manage our growth. One of them has been with me for eleven years. My general manager is my sister, and another project leader is my nephew. He started working for me when I worked out of my home. I had a contract at that time with Kennedy Space Center, and he kind of handled that for me. Not bad to get up and just walk across the hallway to get to the office.

You mentioned fragrance rooms. Is that the biggest distinguishing quality here at your facility?

Yes, the combination of fragrance and laundry. Also, one thing that I did not have [in my old facility] was a test kitchen. I'll now be able to add more of the food vendors and allow them to come and use the kitchen setup that we have. That's a very exciting part of the new building.

What do you do to market your company in this industry?

The majority of my clients come through word of mouth, and many of them are very loyal to me. For instance, one client in particular worked at Pepsi when I met her, then she was with Dell, then another company, then another, and it turns out that she's the best advertisement that I have. A lot of people call me, so it's more like taking orders than it is selling.

It's honest work, and I make it a point to be up front with my clients. If I make a mistake, then I call my clients and tell them I made a mistake. Market research is a very small industry. If you do poor work, it gets out. If you do good work, it gets out. I never thought I'd experience anything where I didn't have to sell, but I haven't had to so far. This year I plan to put together some marketing materials for the first time after four years. Not bad!

Why did you want to own your property instead of continue leasing?

I was throwing away money, and I'd rather have an investment. My plans are to retire in four years, and then I'd like to turn it over to my core team and allow them to take ownership of the company and continue to run it.

I control everything here. Nobody controls me with rent. Nobody says "move this" or "change that." The main thing is that I needed stability and something that we could grow into that will be around for a while.

It seems you think of success not just in the short term, but also how your employees will be affected in the long run.
Yeah, I try to take care of everybody. I pay 100 percent of the benefits of my core team, and 50 percent of the hourly employees' benefits. We also have a 401(k) program in place. If you're not happy in your job and you don't take care of your people, you're not going to earn their loyalty and you won't have longevity. If you want to put out a good product to your client, you have to have a good core team.

Why did you choose Mercantile Commercial Capital for your commercial real estate financing?
When I started my company in 2001 and opened our original location, I didn't have a lot of investors. I ended up maxing out my credit cards and had to deal with that issue. Fortunately, we were able to get out of that debt within a year. I wanted to do this building right, and I didn't want to have the problems I'd had before. Our attorney recommended MCC, and we were offered everything that we needed. You believed in us and were very personable. You (Chris) and Geof [Longstaff] spent a lot of time with us and got very involved. It definitely wasn't your standard

commercial bank where you fill out two mountains of
paperwork and then cross your fingers. MCC worked with
us hand in hand. Overall it was a nice experience, and Geof
has continued to be involved. This building went haywire
during the build-out, and Geof came over just to give me a
hug. I'll never forget that.

What is your fondest memory in your business career?
I had a staff member who started with me when she was in
high school, and she worked with me throughout college.
She went out on her own, and she is now a senior VP of a
company in Ohio. I'm very proud of her. She is a mentor
and a friend, and one of my fondest memories is watching
her grow and develop.

What is the biggest obstacle you've faced?
I've worked with some people who were not very honest
and expressed that they wanted me to "cheat" on certain
projects. I refused to do it, and I quit. It really drove home
my belief that you *have* to be honest to make it in any
business. I've always felt that when I've faced an obstacle,
I either move forward or move around it, so I can't say
anything held me back. The only thing that can hold you
back is yourself. You can do anything.

What's the biggest lesson you've learned?
When dealing with construction, spend a lot of time inter-
viewing your contractor and subcontractors. I was traveling
on business and called in to find out where we stood with
our budget, and they said we were $400,000 over budget. I

got together with my accountant and we were well over the $400,000 mark. I became a construction contractor on the spot. I was Construction Girl during the day and a market researcher at night.

I lost sight, and I got busy. I had hired somebody who was supposed to take care of all this for me. If I had been more involved, I don't think things would have gotten that out of control. We ended up $800,000 over budget. However, Geof was right there to help us through it.

I had trusted somebody fully, and I realize now that I should have been more involved. You have to keep your hands in a little bit of everything as you grow, especially when it's your own business. You can trust people, but still be involved. Always check up on things.

Can you give any advice for small business owners?
Always persevere and work hard. If you are half-hearted about something, don't go into business doing that. If you are not willing to spend your time and money and handle the stress, don't do it. Don't think, "Oh, it would be fun to open a business and run a cookie store," and not realize that you have to get up every morning and run the business. And you always have employees to deal with, and many, many other things to deal with.

Unfortunately, there are no handbooks that say, "*This* is how you start your small business." There are a lot of good books out there, but they won't prepare you for everything.

I recommend a good CPA, a good lawyer, and great bankers to start with. And you must have perseverance. If you go into it half-hearted, it won't work. Put your whole heart into it, and have fun.

We practice the "fish philosophy." Stephen C. Lundin wrote a book called *Fish!* It's about Pike's Fish Market in Seattle, which was going downhill and losing business. The team decided that they could turn it around. One of the key philosophies they adopted is to just have fun. So at Pike's Fish Market, if you ask for salmon, don't be surprised if they run you around and throw your fish back and forth across the store until it finally finds its way into a package so you can take it home. There are a lot of times when we'll turn on some Motown and just sit and talk and have fun and "throw the fish" for a little bit. It's a good way to take a little break and get good, hard work from people.

I've worked in larger corporations all my life. As a manager, I was always criticized for things like having a Friday work-day at my house. My team would come over at 9 a.m. and stay until 5 p.m., when the rest of our families would come over for a barbecue. I found that we were so productive in that one day that we spent together [out of the office environment]. Unfortunately, that's not a normal "corporate" thing to do. This is a company where I can do what I want and I can treat my employees the way I want to—the way they deserve to be treated.

Conclusion

Whatever you can do, or dream you can, begin it.
Boldness has genius, power, and magic in it.
— W. H. Murray

One of these days is none of these days.
—English Proverb

I magine that you are the best widget maker of all time. You had a burning desire to be your own boss, and you had a dream that your widget could change the world. You defied the odds and all the skepticism of your friends and family, and you are carving out a name for yourself in the widget industry.

One morning at 4 a.m., however, you awake and lie there staring at your ceiling. You want to take your widget dreams to even greater heights, but so much of your money is going to your commercial landlord, who is gaining his wealth at your expense. You think about how much better you might do, and how much more wealth you could create for yourself if it weren't for the high rent you have to pay. After all, you could be making those payments to yourself if only you owned the property.

"That's what I did when I bought my house," you think. "No more landlord. Why not do the same for my widget factory?" The next day, you go down to the bank that you've trusted for a decade.

"Sure, we do commercial loans," the banker says. "And you're such a success story that it should glide through our approval process.

We'll take a look at your financials, but figure on, oh, about 25 percent for your down payment, and we'll probably be able to set you up to pay it all off in fifteen years. We'll take care of you."

That could well be where the dream ends. Though you've been successful, how in the world will you come up with that 25 percent? Moreover, instead of paying $5,000 or $6,000 a month in rental payments, you might struggle to pay $7,000 or $8,000 a month in mortgage payments. Sure, you'd be investing in yourself, but what about your business's cash flow? You would be tying up so much of your precious capital that you'd have little left for making ever-better widgets or for that proverbial rainy-day fund, and the loan documents are full of special provisions, requirements that you maintain a specific debt-to-worth ratio and that you make a balloon payment in five-years. All of this makes you fear that your loan could be called one day. You'd be putting your whole livelihood at risk.

This is a picture of what happens on a daily basis in America, but it doesn't have to be that way. There is a far superior alternative to that kind of scenario: the SmartChoice® Commercial Loan. I embrace the idea of owning your own commercial property for your business. I educate people every day about the potential for wealth creation with this strategy. There's a smart way to buy commercial property, and there's a wrong way to do it.

The benefits of the SmartChoice® Commercial Loan are undeniable. In a nutshell, here they are again:

- It requires a third to half the down payment that an ordinary commercial bank loan would require, which means entrepreneurs get to keep their precious capital for better uses. In that way, it fuels smarter business growth.

- The loan terms are much longer than what are offered by conventional lenders, which means monthly payments are less. So this means the loan has less impact on the cash flow of your business, and you're now benefiting yourself, not your landlord.
- Almost half of an SBA 504 loan has the full faith-and-credit guarantee of the U.S. government on it. Often the loan is a full percentage point to 150 basis points below market pricing, yet fixed for an entire twenty years. Not a bank in the country provides such a phenomenal deal outside the SBA 504 structure. It is in this way that it is the least expensive financing vehicle for entrepreneurs who want to buy their commercial real estate.

In the early days of Microsoft, Bill Gates had a mantra that he wanted to put a personal computer on every desk. What I want is for every small business owner in America to have a good opportunity to acquire commercial property in the smartest way possible, and that can be accomplished through the SBA 504 program: the Smart-Choice® Commercial Loan, which is our specialty here at Mercantile.

If you're going to take out an SBA loan, you need to work with someone who knows the loan programs inside and out, focusing on them daily. Otherwise, you're rolling the dice, and if you have a bad experience, you probably rightly only blame yourself for choosing someone less knowledgeable. Perhaps you succumbed to flashy advertising, or just went with the bank you've used for years because that seemed to be the well-worn road, the easier path. Or perhaps you based that decision on the lowest common denominator, the interest rate, just one of many variables that should be included in your buying decision and not even the most important one.

I sometimes ask such borrowers whether they are the lowest-cost provider in their industry. For example, are they the cheapest lawyer, do they make the cheapest widget, are they a cut-rate physician? "Of course not!" they invariably reply, and explain all the factors that set them apart and make them worth what they charge. "Well, I'm better educated, and my widget is more customized and personalized. I give better service and I'm faster than all my competitors, and if something goes wrong with my widget, I'll keep my word and make it right."

When they hear their own words, that's when they usually get it. They *get* that they aren't merely "buying money." They're really buying an entire process; they're buying an experience. It's an experience that they've probably heard can be somewhat painful, and a lot of times it is, but it doesn't have to be. We pride ourselves on making the process as hassle-free as possible for our clients, because it's all we do, and we respect them so highly.

Not everybody offers that respect. Another lender might promise the world but has done little SBA financing. The borrower ends up complaining that the experience was terrible—it took so long; it required so much paperwork; the appraisal was botched. The list of complaints goes on and on. Such experiences contribute to perpetuating those myths I mentioned in the last chapter about SBA lending. If you believe that SBA lenders are all the same and therefore you can go to anyone, you will end up frustrated by the lack of progress.

Alternatively, you could choose a small business lender who could make the experience pleasant, even delightful—a bold step toward your dreams, and in the end, that's what it's all about.

Special Offer for Intrepid Readers

Now that you've finished this book, I hope it's clear that I want you to make the best decision regarding your commercial real estate **for you and your business**. Now may be the right time for you to make the move from renting to owning, or to find a larger facility that will accommodate future growth, but you may also realize that you need to wait. Maybe you need a couple more years of business history under your belt, or you need to get some things in order financially before seriously considering a project like this.

Whether you choose to work with Mercantile or not, I'd like to provide some additional guidance as you wade through the options and possibilities. Here are two bonus offers, just for you:

BONUS #1: A 30-minute one-on-one assessment of your options for commercial property ownership: For up to a half-hour, we'll walk through what your business currently looks like financially and what it would take for you to own your commercial real estate. You'll also have the chance to get answers to any lingering questions you have about the why's and how's of commercial property ownership. Just send an e-mail to info@mercantilecc.com, explaining that you'd like to claim your Bonus Assessment, and we'll get it set up with either myself or one of my senior loan officers (don't tell them I said so, but they're just as good as me at this stuff by now—maybe even better). This is a one-time offer per business, and we'll work with you in advance to make sure we have all the right documents and information so you can get accurate and complete details from this assessment and not waste any of your valuable time.

BONUS #2: Detailed lease vs. own analysis of up to ten commercial properties: Lots of business owners I work with understand the long-term benefits of owning their commercial property, but they still want to know what the immediate impact will be for them. They want to know what the monthly and annual expenses will be so they can decide how affordable a particular commercial property is for them right now. Well, we can do that for you. We can provide you with detailed calculations that show you what it costs to rent instead of own with numerous factors taken into account. We can show you the difference between renting and owning your current commercial property; we can show different scenarios based on estimated lease increases, property appreciation percentages, and so forth; and we can compare multiple different properties (up to ten) so you can see how your options differ in terms of actual costs and potential net worth enhancement. We just need some basic information about the properties you want us to analyze, and we'll crunch the numbers for you. Again, just send an e-mail to info@mercantilecc.com, telling us you'd like to redeem this bonus offer, and we'll get the ball rolling. This is also a one-time offer per business, but it doesn't have to be redeemed at the same time as the above assessment.

Certified Development Companies

As mentioned earlier in this book, Certified Development Companies (CDCs) are the SBA's eyes and ears in local communities across the country. Every SmartChoice® Commercial Loan (aka an SBA 504 loan) requires a CDC to participate. They are the entities that service the second lien position after they've underwritten the credit and received SBA authorization to fund the loan. Frankly, some CDCs are better than others, as you can well imagine. Below is a list (by state) of some of the best in the country. We've had the pleasure, at MCC, to work with approximately eighty of them. This is not an exhaustive list as there are about 110 others, but if you want to communicate with a CDC, I've given you their basic contact details here. In most cases where you've applied for an SBA 504 loan, your lender (the entity that will hopefully provide the first lien position) will recommend the appropriate CDC they want to work with on your project. This is not something you must normally investigate yourself, but now you have all the information you need on the following pages.

ALABAMA

Alabama Small Business Capital
3120 Frederick Road, Suite K
Opelika, AL 36801
(334) 318-8064
www.fbdc.net

Alacom Finance
117 Southcrest Drive, Suite 100
Birmingham, AL 35209
(205) 942-3360
www.clacom.com

Greater Mobile Development Corporation
1301 Azalea Road
Mobile, AL 36693
(251) 650-0826
www.greatermobile.org

Southern Development Council
8132 Old Federal Road
Montgomery, AL 36117
(334) 244-1801
www.sdcinc.org

ALASKA

Evergreen Business Capital
P.O. Box 3673
Palmer, AK 99645
(907) 746-5047
www.evergreen504.com

ARIZONA

Business Development Finance Corporation
3300 N. Central Avenue, Suite 600
Phoenix, AZ 85012
(602) 381-6292
www.bdfc.com

Southwestern Business Financing Corporation
3200 N. Central Avenue, Suite 1550
Phoenix, AZ 85012
(602) 495-6495
www.swbfc.com

ARKANSAS

Six Bridges Capital Corporation
200 River Market Ave., Suite 400
Little Rock, AR 72201
(501) 374-9247
www.accglending.com

West Central Arkansas Planning Development District
P.O. Box 6409
Hot Springs, AR 71902
(501) 525-7577
www.wcapdd.dina.org

CALIFORNIA

Advantage CDC
11 Golden Shore, Suite 630
Long Beach, CA 90802
(562) 983-7450
www.advantagecdc.org

Arcata Economic Development Corporation
100 Ericson Court, Suite 100A
Arcata, CA 95521
(707) 822-4616
www.aedc1.org

California Statewide CDC
426 D Street
Davis, CA 95616
(530) 756-9310
www.calstatewide.com

Capital Funding
5428 Watt Avenue
North Highlands, CA 95660
(916) 339-1096
www.gscdc.com

CDC Small Business Finance
2448 Historic Decatur Road, Suite 200
San Diego, CA 92106
(619) 243-8610
www.cdcloans.com

Coastal Business Finance
930 South Broadway, Suite 101
Santa Maria, CA 93454
(805) 739-1665
www.coastalbusinessfinance.com

EDF Resource Capital
1050 Iron Point Road
Folsom, CA 95630
(916) 962-3669
www.resourcecapital.com

Landmark Certified Development Corporation
441 E. Whittier Blvd, Suite C
La Habra, CA 90631
(562) 690-6400
www.landmarkcdc.org

Los Angeles LDC
1200 Wilshire Blvd, Suite 404
Los Angeles, CA 90017
(213) 362-9113
www.losangelesldc.com

Mid-State Development Corporation
5555 California Avenue, Suite 105
Bakersfield, CA 93309
(661) 322-4241
www.msdcdc.org

San Fernando Valley Small Business Development Corporation
5121 Van Nuys Blvd, 3rd Floor
Van Nuys, CA 91403
(818) 205-1770
www.ssvfdc.org

Southland EDC
400 N. Tustin Avenue, Suite 125
Santa Ana, CA 92705
(714) 647-1143
www.southlandedc.com

Success Capital EDC
1420 F. Street, 2nd Floor
Modesto, CA 95354
(209) 521-9372
www.seedco.org

TMC Financing
440 Pacific Avenue
San Francisco, CA 94133
(415) 989-8855
www.tmcfinancing.com

COLORADO

CEDCO Small Business Finance Corporation
1175 Osage Street, Suite 110
Denver, CO 80204
(303) 893-8989
www.cedco.org

Colorado Lending Source
518 17th Street, Unit 1800
Denver, CO 80202
(303) 657-0010
www.coloradolendingsource.org

Pikes Peak Regional Development Corporation
322 S. Cascade Avenue
Colorado Springs, CO 80903
(719) 471-2044
www.pprdc.com

Preferred Lending Partners
140 East 19th Avenue, Suite 202
Denver, CO 80203
(303) 861-4100
www.preferredlendingpartners.net

SCEDD Development Company
The Business Lending Center
1104 North Main Street
Pueblo, CO 81003
(719) 545-8680
www.scedd.com

CONNECTICUT

Connecticut Business Development Corp
1224 Mills Street, Building B
East Berlin, CT 06023
(860) 828-2135

Connecticut Community Investment Corporation
2315 Whitney Avenue, Suite 2B
Hamden, CT 06518
(203) 776-6172
www.ctcic.org

DELAWARE

Delaware Community Development Corporation
100 West 10th Street, Suite 706
Wilmington, DE 19801
(302) 571-9088
www.wedco.org

DISTRICT OF COLUMBIA

Chesapeake Business Finance Corp.
1101 30th St NW, Suite 500
Washington, DC 20007
(202) 625-4373
www.chesapeake504.com

FLORIDA

Florida Business Development Corporation
6801 Lake Worth Road, Suite 209
Lake Worth, FL 33467
(561) 433-0233
www.fbdc.net

Florida First Capital Finance Corporation
1351 N. Gadsden
Tallahassee, FL 32303
(850) 681-3601
www.ffcfc.com

GulfCoast Business Finance, Inc.
227 2nd Avenue North
St. Petersburg, FL 33701
(727) 895-2504
www.gulfcoastbiz.com

GEORGIA

Capital Partners CDC
6445 Powers Ferry Road, Suite 210
Atlanta, GA 30339
(404) 475-6000
www.cpcdc.com

GA REsource Capital
5400 Laurel Springs Parkway, Bldg. 800,
Suite 802
Suwanee, GA 30024
(770) 205-9800
www.ga.resourcecapital.com

**Georgia Certified Development
Corporation**
3405 Piedmont Road, Suite 500
Atlanta, GA 30305
(404) 442-2480
www.gacdc.com

NGCDC, Inc.
P.O. Box 1798
Rome, GA 30162
(706) 295-6485
www.ngcdc.org

Small Business Access Partners
460 South Enota Drive
Gainsville, GA 30501
(770) 536-7839
www.sbaploans.com

HAWAII

**Hawaii Community Reinvestment
Corporation**
3465 Waialae Ave, Suite 393
Honolulu, HI 96816
(808) 532-3110
www.hcrc-hawaii.org

**HEDCO Local Development
Corporation**
222 S. Vineyard St. PH-1
Honolulu, HI 96813
(808) 521-6502
www.hedcoldc.com

Lokahi Pacific Rural Development
1935 Main Street, Suite 204
Wailuku, HI 96793
(808) 242-5761
www.lokahipacific.org

IDAHO

Business Lending Solutions
P.O. Box 5079
Twin Falls, ID 83303
(208) 732-5730
www.businesslendingsolutions.org

Panhandle Area Council, Inc.
11100 N. Airport Drive
Hayden, ID 83835
(208) 772-0584
www.pacni.org

The Development Company
299 East 4th North
Rexburg, ID 83440
(208) 356-4524
www.thedevco.net

ILLINOIS

CenterPoint 504
One University Parkway, Room C3300
University Park, IL 60484
(708) 534-4928
www.cp504.com

Illinois Business Financial Services
411 Hamilton Blvd, Suite 1330
Peoria, IL 61602
(309) 495-5976
www.ibfs.org

Lake County Partnership for Economic Development
28055 Ashley Circle, Suite 212
Libertyville, IL 60048
(847) 247-0137
www.lakecountypartners.com

Rockford Local Development Corporation
120 W. State Street, Suite 306
Rockford. IL 61101
(815) 987-8675
www.rldc.us

Small Business Growth Corporation
2401 W. White Oaks Drive
Springfield, IL 62704
(217) 787-7557
www.growthcorp.com

SomerCor 504, Inc.
601 South LaSalle, Suite 510
Chicago, IL 60605
(312) 360-3312
www.somercor.com

INDIANA

Regional Development Company
1757 Thornapple Circle
Valparaiso, IN 46385
(219) 476-0504
www.rdc504.org

The Community Development Corporation of Northeast Indiana
Citizens Square 200 East Berry Street,
Suite 320
Fort Wayne, IN 46802
(260) 427-1127
www.cdcnein.org

IOWA

Black Hawk Economic Development, Inc.
3835 W. 9th Street
Waterloo, IA 50702
(319) 235-2960
www.bhed.org

Corporation for Economic Development in Des Moines
400 Robert D. Ray Drive
Des Moines, IA 50309
(515) 283-4017
www.ceddm.com

E.C.I.A. Business Growth, Inc.
7600 Commerce Park
Dubuque, IA 52002
(563) 556-4166
www.eciabusinessgrowth.com

Siouxland Economic Development Corporation
1106 Historic 4th Street, Suite 201
Sioux City, IA 51101
(712) 279-6430
www.siouxlandedc.com

KANSAS

Frontier Financial Partners, Inc.
1512 West 6th Ave, Suite E
Emporia, KS 66801
(620) 342-7041
www.frontierfinancialpartners.com

Great Plains Development, Inc.
P.O. Box 1116
Dodge City, KS 67801
(620) 227-6406
www.gpdionline.com

Heartland Business Capital
8900 Indian Creek Parkway, Suite 150
Overland Park, KS 66210
(913) 599-1717
www.hbcloans.com

Mid-America CDC
Pittsburg State University 1701 S. Broadway
Pittsburg, KS 66762
(620) 235-4924
www.btikansas.com

Pioneer Country Development
P.O. Box 248
Hill City, KS 67642
(785) 421-3488
www.rookscounty.net

KENTUCKY

Capital Access Corporation- Kentucky
401 West Main Street, Suite 2010
Louisville, KY 40202
(502) 584-2175
www.cac-ky.org

Community Ventures Corporation
1450 North Broadway
Lexington, KY 40505
(859) 231-0054
www.cvcky.org

LOUISIANA

Regional Loan Corporation
330 Camp Street
New Orleans, LA 70130
(504) 524-6172
www.rlcsbidco.com

MARYLAND

Mid-Atlantic Business Finance Company
1410 N. Crain Highway, Suite 5B
Glen Burnie, MD 21061
(410) 863-1600
www.mabfc.com

Prince George's Financial Services Corporation
1100 Mercantile Lane, Suite 115-A
Largo, MD 20774
(301) 883-6900

MICHIGAN

Economic Development Foundation
1345 Monroe NW, Suite 132
Grand Rapids, MI 49505
(616) 459-4825
www.growmichigan.com

Metropolitan Growth & Development Corporation15100 Northline Road,
Suite 133
Southgate, MI 48195
(734) 362-3447

Michigan Certified Development Corporation
3737 Coolidge Road, Suite 2
East Lansing, MI 48823
(517) 886-6612
www.michigancdc.org

SEM Resource Capital
17199 N. Laurel Park Dr., Suite 300
Livonia, MI 48152
(734) 464-4418
www.sem.resourcecapital.com

MINNESOTA

504 Corporation
220 South Broadway, Suite 100
Rochester, MN 55904
(507) 288-6442
www.504corporation.com

Central Minnesota Development Company
1885 Station Parkway, NW
Andover, MN 55304
(763) 784-3337
www.cmdcbusinessloans.com

Minnesota Business Finance Corporation
616 Roosevelt Road, Suite 200
St. Cloud, MN 56301
(320) 258-5000
www.mbfc.org

SPEDCO
3900 Northwoods Drive, Suite 225
Arden Hills, MN 55112
(651) 631-4900
www.spedco.com

Twin Cities-Metro CDC
3495 Vadnais Center Drive
Vadnais Heights, MN 55110
1-888-481-4504
www.504lending.com

MISSISSIPPI

Central Mississippi Development Company, Inc.
P.O. Box 4935
Jackson, MS 39296
(601) 981-1511
www.cmpdd.org

Three Rivers Local Development Company
P.O. Box 690
Pontotoc, MS 38863
(662) 489-2415
www.trpdd.com

MISSOURI

Business Finance Corporation of St. Louis County
121 S. Meramec, Suite 900
St. Louis, MO 63105
(314) 615-7663
www.slcec.com

Economic Development Corporation of Jefferson County
P.O. Box 623
Hillsboro, MO 63050
(636) 797-5336
www.jeffcountymo.org

EDC Loan Corporation
1100 Walnut Street, Suite 1700
Kansas City, MO 64106
(816) 691-2111
www.edckc.com

Enterprise Development Corporation
910 E. Broadway, Suite 201
Columbia, MO 65201
(573) 875-8117
www.entdevcorp.org

Meramec Regional Development Corporation
4 Industrial Drive
St. James, MO 65559
(573) 265-2993
www.meramecregion.org

Midwest Small Business Finance
1251 NW Briarcliff Parkway, Suite 25
Kansas City, MO 64116
(816) 468-4989
www.simplymoreloans.com

RMI
3324 Emerald Lane
Jefferson City, MO 65109
(573) 635-0136
www.rmiinc.org

St. Louis Development Corporation
1520 Market Street, Suite 2000
St. Louis, MO 63101
(314) 657-3700
www.StLouis-Mo.gov

MONTANA

High Plains Financial
P.O. Box 949
Great Falls, MT 59403
(406) 454-1934
www.gfdevelopment.org

NEBRASKA

Community Development Resources
285 S. 68th Street Place, Suite 520
Lincoln, NE 68510
(402) 436-2387
www.cdr-nebraska.org

NEDCO
1610 S. 70th Street, Suite 201
Lincoln, NE 68506
(402) 483-4600
www.nedcoloans.org

NEVADA

Nevada State Development Corporation
1551 Desert Crossing Court, Suite 100
Las Vegas, NV 89144
(702) 877-9111
www.nsdc-loans.com

New Ventures Capital Development Company
626 S. 9th Street
Las Vegas, NV 89101
(702) 382-9522
www.newventurescdc.com

NEW HAMPSHIRE

Capital Regional Development Council
P.O. Box 664
Concord, NH 03302
(603) 228-1872
www.crdc-nh.com

NEW JERSEY

Across Nations Pioneers, Inc.
15 Engle Street, Suite 107
Englewood, NJ 07631
(201) 541-4101
www.acrossnations.org

New Jersey Business Finance Corporation
2050 Center Avenue, Suite 375
Fort Lee, NJ 07024
(201) 346-0300
www.njbfc.com

Regional Business Assistance Corporation
3111 Quakerbridge Road, 2nd Floor
Mercerville, NJ 08619
(609) 587-1133
www.rbacloan.com

NEW MEXICO

Enchantment Land CDC
625 Silver Avenue SW, Suite 195
Albuquerque, NM 87102
(505) 843-9232
www.elcdc.com

NEW YORK

Business Initiative Corporation of New York
The Bronx County Building
851 Grand Concourse, Suite 123
Bronx, NY 10451
(718) 590-3980

Empire State Certified Development Corporation
50 Beaver Street, Suite 600
Albany, NY 12207
(518) 463-2268
www.nybdc.com

Long Island Development Corporation
400 Post Avenue, Suite 201A
Westberry, NY 11590
(516) 433-5000
www.lidc.org

NORTH CAROLINA

Avista Business Development Corporation
P.O. Box 7032
Asheville, NC 28802
(828) 645-0439
www.avistabdc.com

Business Expansion Funding Corporation
5970 Fairview Road, Suite 218
Charlotte, NC 28210
(704) 442-8145
www.befcor.com

Centralina Development Corporation
P.O. Box 34218
Charlotte, NC 28234
(704) 373-1233
www.centralinacapital.com

Neuse River Development Authority, Inc.
P.O. Box 1111
New Bern, NC 28563
(252) 638-6724
www.nrda.org

Self-Help Ventures Fund
P.O. Box 3619
Durham, NC 27702
(919) 956-4473
www.self-help.org

NORTH DAKOTA

Lake Agassiz Certified Development Corporation
417 Main Avenue
Fargo, ND 58103
(701) 235-1197
www.lakeagassizcdc.com

Lewis & Clark CDC
200 1st Avenue NW, Suite 100
Mandan, ND 58554
(701) 667-7620
www.lewisandclarkcdc.org

OHIO

Access Business Development & Finance, Inc.
7370 Liberty One Drive
Liberty Township, OH 45044
(513) 777-2225
www.accessbdf.com

Cascade Capital Corporation
1 Cascade Plaza, 18th Floor
Akron, OH 44308
(330) 379-3160
www.cascadecapital.org

Clark County Development Corporation
300 East Auburn Avenue
Springfield, OH 45505
(937) 322-8685

Community Capital Development Corporation
900 Michigan Avenue
Columbus, OH 43215
(614) 645-6171
www.ccdcorp.org

CountyCorp Development
130 W. 2nd Street, Suite 1420
Dayton, OH 45402
(937) 225-6328
www.countycorp.com

Growth Capital Corp
1360 East Ninth Street, Suite 350
Cleveland, OH 44114
(216) 592-2332
www.growthcapitalcorp.com

Horizon Certified Development Company
1776 Mentor Avenue
Cincinnati, OH 45212
(513) 631-8292
www.hcdc.com

Lake County Small Business Assistance Corporation
1 Victoria Place
Painsville, OH 44077
(440) 357-2290
www.lcport.org

Mahoning Valley EDC
4319 Belmont Avenue
Youngstown, OH 44505
(330) 759-3668
www.mvedc.com

Mentor Economic Assistance Corporation
8500 Civic Center Blvd
Mentor, OH 44060
(440) 974-5739
www.meacoweb.com

OKLAHOMA

Metro Area Development Corporation
6412 N. Santa Fe Avenue, Suite C
Oklahoma City, OK 73116
(405) 424-5181
www.madco.net

Tulsa Economic Development Corporation
907 S. Detroit Avenue
Tulsa, OK 74120
(918) 585-8332
www.tulsaedc.com

OREGON

Cascades West Financial Services, Inc.
494 State Street, Suite 270
Salem, OR 97301
(503) 990-6868
www.cascadeswest.com

Greater Eastern Oregon Development Corporation
P.O. Box 1041
Pendleton, OR 97801
(541) 276-6745
www.geodc.net

Oregon Business Development Corporation
334 NE Hawthorne Avenue
Bend, OR 97701
(541) 548-9538
www.oregonbusinessdevelopment.org

PENNSYLVANIA

Altoona-Blair County Development Corporation
3900 Industrial Park Drive
Altoona, PA 16602
(814) 944-6113
www.abcdcorp.org

Bridgeway Capital CDC
707 Grant Street, Suite 1920
Pittsburgh, PA 15219
(412) 201-2450
www.bridgewaycapital.org

DelVal Business Finance Corp.
6100 City Avenue, Suite P218
Philadelphia, PA 19131
(215) 871-3770
www.delval504.com

Lehigh Valley Economic Development Corporation
2158 Avenue C
Bethlehem, PA 18017
(610) 266-6775
www.lehighvalley.org

Pennsylvania Community Development & Finance Corporation
2561 Bernville Road
Reading, PA 19605
(610) 898-6045
www.pcdfc.com

Seedcopa
737 Constitution Drive
Exton, PA 19341
(610) 321-8242
www.seedcopa.com

SOUTH CAROLINA

Appalachian Development Corporation
3531 Pelham Road, Suite 100
Greenville, SC 29615
(864) 382-2350
www.appalachiandevelopmentcorp.com

CDC of South Carolina
P.O. Box 21823
Columbia, SC 29221
(803) 744-0303
www.businessdevelopment.org

Provident Business Financial Services, Inc.
3937 Sunset Blvd, Suite D
West Columbia, SC 29169
(803) 233-6386
www.providentbfs.com

SOUTH DAKOTA

Black Hills Community Economic Development, Inc.
525 University Loop, Suite 102
Rapid City, SD 57701
(605) 347-5837
www.bhced.org

Dakota Business Finance
500 N. Western Avenue, Suite 100
Sioux Falls, SD 57104
(605) 367-5353
www.dakotabusinessfinance.com

First District Development Company
124 1st Avenue NW/P.O. Box 1207
Watertown, SD 57201
(605) 882-5115
www.1stdistrict.org

TENNESSEE

Brightbridge, Inc.
P.O. Box 871
Chattanooga, TN 37401
(423) 424-4220
www.brightbridgeinc.org

**Mid-Cumberland Area Development
Corporation (MADC)**
501 Union Street, 6th Floor
Nashville, TN 37219
(615) 862-8866
www.madc.us

**Tennessee Business Development
Corporation**
1301 E. Wood Street, Suite 2
Paris, TN 38242
(731) 644-1335

TEXAS

ACCION Texas, Inc.
2014 S. Hackberry Street
San Antonio, TX 78210
(210) 226-3664
www.acciontexas.org

Alliance Lending Corporation
3030 LBJ Freeway, Suite 700
Dallas, TX 75234
(214) 722-7512
www.alliancecdc.com

Capital CDC
1250 South Capital of Texas Highway
Building 1, Suite 600
Austin, Texas 78746
(512) 327-9229
www.CapitalCDC.com

**Community Certified Development
Corporation**
8590 Highway 6 North
Houston, TX 77095
(713) 457-1650
www.communitycdc.com

Dallas Business Finance Corporation
400 Zang Blvd, Suite 1210
Dallas, TX 75208
(214) 948-7800
www.sddc.org

Greater Texas Capital Corp.
3600 Old Bullard Road, Suite 403
Tyler, TX 75701
(903) 535-9229
www.getcdc.org

Texas Panhandle Regional Development Corporation
801 South Fillmore, Suite 205
Amarillo, TX 79101
(806) 331-6172
www.amarilloedc.com

UTAH

Utah CDC
5333 S. Adams Avenue, Suite B
Ogden, UT 84405
(801) 627-1333
www.utahcdc.com

VERMONT

Northern Community Investment Corporation
347 Portland Street
St. Johnsbury, VT 05819
(802) 748-5101
www.ncic.org

Vermont 504 Corporation
58 East State Street, Suite 5
Montpelier, VT 05602
(802) 828-5627
www.veda.org

VIRGINIA

Crater Development Company
1964 Wakefield Street
P.O. Box 1808
Petersburg, VA 23805
(804) 861-1666
www.craterpdc.org

REDCO 504
1125 Jefferson Davis Highway, Suite 420
Fredericksburg, VA 22404
(540) 373-2897
www.redco504.org

REDC Community Capital Group, Inc.
411 East Franklin Street, Suite 203
Richmond, VA 23219
(804) 780-3012
www.redcfinance.org

Tidewater Business Financing Corporation
500 E. Main Street, Suite 403
Norfolk, VA 23510
(757) 623-2691
www.tidewaterbusinessfinancing.com

WASHINGTON

Ameritrust CDC
11050 5th Avenue NE, Suite 205
Seattle, WA 98125
(206) 402-3971
www.ameritrustcdc.com

Evergreen Business Capital
13925 Interurban Avenue South, Suite 100
Seattle, WA 98168
1-800-878-6613
www.evergreen504.com

Northwest Business Development Association
9019 E. Appleway Blvd, Suite 200
Spokane Valley, WA 99212
(509) 458-8555
www.nwbusiness.org

WEST VIRGINIA

OVIBDC CDC, Inc.
1310 Market Street, Third Floor
P.O. Box 1029
Wheeling, WV 26003
(304) 232-7722

WISCONSIN

Great Lakes Asset Corporation
200 South Washington Street
Green Bay, WI 54301
(920) 499-6444
www.greatlakesasset.com

Impact Seven
147 Almena Drive
Almena, WI 54805
(715) 357-3334
www.impactseven.org

Wisconsin Business Development
Finance Corporation
P.O. Box 2717
Madison, WI 53701
(608) 819-0390
www.wbd.org

WYOMING

WIDC-Frontier CDC
232 East Second Street, Suite 300
Casper, WY 82601
(307) 234-5351
www.widcfrontier.com

Commercial Real Estate Brokers

In Chapter Three I talked about why it's important to choose the right commercial real estate broker for your unique project. I also gave some practical ways to go about doing that, and mentioned that some of the larger commercial real estate brokerages may be helpful because they have tons of resources at their disposal. In this case, being big is a good thing, because these companies are able to have locally-focused offices to serve particular geographic areas (possibly like yours) that also have specialized commercial brokers (industrial, office, retail, etc.). On the following pages is a list of large, national commercial brokerage firms (in alphabetical order) that Mercantile Capital Corporation has worked with. The primary, corporate website is listed for each company, so you'll want to find the local office near you (which may have a locally-focused website of its own). While I can't guarantee you'll find the "right" commercial real estate broker at any one of these companies—and this list is by no means finite—we've had very good experiences with them in the past, and these are great places to start.

Cassidy Turley
www.cassidyturley.com

CBRE
www.cbre.com

Coldwell Banker Commercial
www.cbcworldwide.com

Colliers International
www.colliers.com

Cushman and Wakefield
www.cushwake.com

Lee & Associates
www.lee-associates.com

Marcus & Millichap
www.marcusmillichap.com

NAI Global
www.naiglobal.com

Newmark Grubb Knight Frank
www.newmarkkf.com

Sperry Van Ness
www.svn.com

I also mentioned earlier in this book that paying attention to profes-sional designations may help you find the right commercial real estate broker. The two most prominent designations to look for are CCIM (Certified Commercial Investment Member) and SIOR (Society of Industrial and Office Realtors). Below is contact information for each of these organizations so you can find out more:

CCIM Institute
430 Michigan Avenue, Suite 800
Chicago, IL 60611
(800) 621-7027
www.ccim.com

SIOR
1201 New York Avenue, NW, Suite 350
Washington, DC 20005
(202) 449-8200
www.sior.com

Other Business Books in Which I've Appeared

I've been asked by others to contribute chapters to their books as a guest author on several occasions. I've also been quoted and/or featured in a case study more than once. The following is a list of these books in which you'll find my name listed as a contributor in some way, shape, or form. If you're so inclined, I'd encourage you to check them out:

No B.S. Wealth Attraction in the New Economy by Dan Kennedy

Money, Money Everywhere but Not a Drop for Main Street by Bob Coleman

Uncensored Sales Strategies: A Radical New Approach to Selling Your Customers What They Really Want—No Matter What Business You're In by Sydney Biddle Barrows

Big Ideas for Your Business by America's Premiere Experts

The Insider Secrets: To Get Money to Grow Your Business by Nate Kennedy

No B.S. Marketing to the Affluent by Dan Kennedy

How to Make Maximum Money with Minimum Customers by Craig Garber

No B.S. Ruthless Management of People and Profits by Dan Kennedy

Secrets to Growing Your Veterinary Practice in the New Economy by Dean Biggs

The Insider Secrets of the World's Most Successful Mortgage Brokers by Nate Kennedy

The A-List Salon: Insider Secrets of Profitable Salons that Wow Their Clients Every Day by Veronica Wood—forthcoming

No B.S. Marketing to Seniors and Leading Edge Boomers by Dan Kennedy—forthcoming

You Can Do It

The following are comments from small business owners who have worked with Mercantile to apply the principles and strategies described in this book. I've put them here for you to read so you know that this is all very doable, and that it's possible to have a positive (hopefully even enjoyable) experience with your commercial lender. If these folks can do it, you can do it, too. Whether or not you work with Mercantile at any point in the future, I hope the information you've read in this book is helpful and makes a difference for your wealth and your business. Now, here's what some of our Clients have said:

....

"I discovered MCC online, searching for SBA lenders. What made all the difference for me was their ability to very quickly review my business plan, my forecast financials, and to confidently state that 'this is not a problem, we can do this deal.' There are a lot of things to manage in order to close a loan, but I didn't deal with any of it. And I was really only called if something was needed from me, and that just made it a pleasure. That made it so efficient, and it eliminated a lot of headaches. The communications process was really streamlined for me. I would absolutely recommend MCC to anyone thinking about owning commercial property. I would work with them again myself, and that's the strongest endorsement that I can give."

ANDREW MARTIN, Owner and Founder
Serene Center
Long Beach, CA
www.serenecenter.com

"We went with the SmartChoice® Commercial Loan Program because it was a no brainer. We believe that owning our building is important because we don't want to throw our hard earned money away to landlords when we should be building equity in our company. MCC provided us with that opportunity, and to finance the business at very low costs and a reasonable down payment. Another benefit of the program is that were we able to finance the improvements that we needed to make to bring the childcare facilities up to our expectations and requirements. It feels good to know that when we retire we have an asset that we built and we can sell our facilities at that time. MCC has given us the opportunity to do more sooner than we thought we could do. They were such a perfect partner for us that with their help we were able to get four locations up and running within two years, which exceeded all our expectations."

LANCE STEMPLES, Owner
Leaps and Bounds Learning Center
Edgewater, FL
lblc.org

"I talked to 20 different banks until I found MCC, and they got to work on my loan quickly. The process was not without its bumps, but MCC continued to encourage and reassure us that we were going to get this deal done. They really know what they're doing, and I wouldn't want anybody else working for me when it comes to dealing with the SBA."

DAVE DENTI, Owner
Max & Erma's
Chillicothe, Findlay, and Lancaster, OH
maxandermas.com

"Banks don't like financing grocery stores even in best of times, so who wants to finance commercial construction, single use building with a large capital cost of equipment in today's market? No one! Three years ago if you had talked to me about doing an SBA loan, I would have laughed and said 'no way.' But, today, with historical low interest rates and the ability to finance the building and equipment with a fixed rate for 20 plus years, you would be crazy not to do it! Mercantile has a team that understands small businesses and their needs. They are experts at the 504 loan program. If you are a small business owner like me, who has been banging at the door of banks and not getting anywhere, give them a call. It might just be your lucky day."

Nakul & Nisha Patel, Co-Owners
Mt. Plymouth IGA
Sorrento, FL
mtplymouthiga.com

"We can't thank Mercantile Capital enough for the successful acquisition of our new property and build-out of our restaurant. Mercantile provided us the necessary guidance and support which resulted in a very smooth acquisition. The SBA 504 loan program has not only provided us with tax and appreciation benefits on the real estate, but has also locked in occupancy rates for the long term. We will definitely be working with Mercantile Capital again this year as we continue to grow."

Bo & Brody Bennett, Owners
Jimmy John's Gourmet Sandwich Shop
Chandler, AZ

"What I learned in dealing with MCC is that the SBA process, particularly for new construction, is a very specialized program that cannot be handled by amateurs. I was most impressed with MCC's ability to define and focus on the specifics, as well as the efforts put forth in leading me through the maze. Never did MCC leave me dangling or in question of answers that I needed to generate. I have never worked with a lender who so consciously strove to work with its clients in not only the front-end underwriting, but the actual administration of the loans and construction draws as well. MCC is a credit to the lending industry, and more so to the SBA, as an example of what professionalism and intelligent business service can provide."

Howard B. Lefkowitz, Owner, President and CEO
Leeds Holdings Southeast, Inc.
Winter Park, FL
leedsholdings.com

"Had it not been for Mercantile Capital Corporation's tremendous skill, speed, expertise, and availability, I truly believe our loan would not have closed. In a lending environment where bankers kick their feet up on the desk and look down their nose at small businesses, your company treated our financial needs with the dignity and respect they deserved. We would and will recommend your services in the future!"

Mo Dari, Owner
The Oasis Restaurant & Delivery
Toledo, OH
eatatoasis.com

"We actually own our property through a separate entity. We felt, in this particular situation, we would be well-served by using this as a long-term investment. So it was really an investment vehicle for our shareholders. We looked at other opportunities, other vendors of financial services, and it seems like the 504 loan package was the best we could put together. MCC provided the best overall package, the most creative and unique approach, and they handled everything very well. Frankly, at the time we were doing it, they were fairly new in the business, but it was all handled very well. I'm sure it was a complex financing vehicle, but they made it very simple for us. The paperwork involved was even less than when I refinanced my home loan. We always felt very well informed about what was occurring or what would occur next."

John Benz, Chairman
TLC Engineering for Architecture
Orlando, FL
tlc-engineers.com

"MCC was the only reason I was able to navigate through the difficult SBA 504 process. Their knowledge was key to closing the loan. Their client service was exceptional, something that I demand from others but rarely receive. I will recommend their firm to many, many future clients of MCC. The obstacles in acquiring this loan were enormous. Until I first spoke with them, I tried unsuccessfully for eight months to find a banker who understood the 504 process. They were the guys who made it happen."

Dan Dennis, Owner
Dennis Corporation
Columbia, SC
denniscorporation.com

"I first approached MCC after being referred to them for their high quality customer service and quick, creative underwriting. They quickly and honestly advised me that my project was too ambitious based on the performance of my company at that time, but also said that they would be happy to work with me if I scaled the project back. I was determined to see my vision through so I proceeded to waste nearly twelve months being strung-along by two other lenders who told me what I wanted to hear, but could not come through. I eventually went back to MCC, in part because they had been right and were so quick to come to their conclusion in the first place. My business operations had continued to grow and based on my progress, MCC quickly approved me for an even larger construction-to-permanent loan than the one I had originally sought. It's truly ironic and funny how all of this worked out. I probably could not have done this without the honest, fast feedback and professionalism of MCC. I am truly grateful and look forward to building more locations with them soon."

> **MATT DeMIKE**, Owner
> Boardwalk Pizza
> Winter Park, FL
> boardwalkpizza.com

"Mercantile worked very hard to make this refinance happen. It was a complex loan structure and large refinance amount. At a time when hotel financing is challenging for borrowers, I am very glad that Mercantile was able to help me to pay off my original loan that was already matured and on a short-term extension."

> **KIRAN PATEL**, Owner
> Country Inn & Suites
> Capitol Heights, MD
> countryinns.com

"We bought back the business not long before looking at purchasing commercial property. We used some cash doing so and didn't want to get into a situation where we had to put 25% down. Other lending institutions were looking at us as a new business because we only gave them two years of tax returns. Chris, instead of just telling me 'No,' figured out what we needed to do to get a 'Yes.' We ended up having to put down 15% instead of 10%, but it gave me the fixed product I was looking for, with the least amount of money down, with longer terms. There were a couple of changes that happened during the process including the turn lane that we had to work with a couple of the other building owners in the immediate vicinity. Geof and Chris helped us work through that process.

Quite frankly, I don't know if anyone else would have helped us with that. Once the loan was closed they would have gone away and said it was our problem to deal with. This building is our retirement program. We now have a retirement program independent of the business. The business is the icing on the cake."

KEITH KEMP, Co-Owner
Xerographic Digital Printing
Orlando, FL
xerocopy.com

"If I had to go through the SBA 504 loan process again, I would do an instant replay. Everybody at Mercantile Capital Corporation really cares and wants to see small business owners advance to the next level of commercial property ownership. They were very friendly and diligent in processing my loan, doing everything they could to get my project up and running."

DARLENE ANDERSON, Owner
Bundles of Joy Learning Center
Champaign, IL

"It's important as a business owner to own your own building simply because you're not wasting money. It's not money thrown out on rent. It's part of your own investment and you keep it to yourself. So, when you're working hard and you're paying the mortgage you know it's for yourself and you're securing your future. Mercantile Capital offered so much information. When I came to them I didn't know the process or which way to go. Learning what the forms are, and what the process is, was a full education because in the beginning you just don't know all these things. But what impressed me the most about Chris, from the first moment I spoke with him, was his patience. His explanation of the process really gave me a feeling of comfort that this was a done deal. Chris made it happen. This project meant so much for my company. It made me strong and anchored me in a beautiful place. I now have an area where I can entertain my clients. It's a place where I can bring them in and, say, sign a contract. It's a beautiful environment. It gives you strength as a business person that you don't get working out of your home. Knowing that you're doing it for yourself and that it's yours, no one else's, makes it even better. MCC holds your hand through the process. I love the facility and the fact that the money I put into it is mine. It's like owning your own home. You just have to take the step to do it and associate yourself with the right people to do it with."

EDDIE DIAZ, Event Producer and CEO
Encore Creations
Orlando, FL
encorecreations.com

"I am so happy to finally own the center that I have been operating in for 13 years, and to no longer deal with landlord challenges. This could not have happened without the help of Mercantile, and I am just so thankful."

HAILE DEGENA, Owner
Royal Wine, Spirits & Food
Denver, CO

"MCC made it easy for us to own our commercial property rather than lease it. We were able to finance not only the real estate, but also FF&E (furniture, fixtures & equipment) and closing costs. This helped a great deal. In addition to this, MCC was more than helpful through a very tough situation for us. My brother in-law (and a principal in our company) passed away during the ground-up construction of our building. The MCC loan officers and staff in their closing department helped guide us through the rest of the process without missing a beat. This project could not have been completed without their expertise and willingness to go the extra mile for us. We will certainly use MCC for our future financing needs."

TOM MASSON, Principal
Dunkin Donuts/Baskin Robins
Bushnell, FL

"At the start of the loan process, everyone told me it would be impossible to get an SBA loan. Mercantile Capital got me the loan ahead of our schedule and with little hassle. The tough economy didn't stop them from getting us our SBA loan and achieving our 20-year goal of owning our restaurant property."

DAVID ZISLIS, Co-Owner
Manhattan Beach Brewing Company, Inc.
Manhattan Beach, CA
brewcomb.com

"Owning commercial property gives me a strong sense of financial security. I am an optometrist, and I wanted to own the property my practice occupies for retirement purposes. Valuations on private practices have been dwindling in the last couple of decades so I knew I needed more than just the sale of my practice to retire on. I'm also in a position to develop the 2.1 acres I own and lease, or sell new buildings or pads. The door of financial opportunity is now wide open for years to come. I owe a great deal to MCC for assisting me in the acquisition. I am a young professional and did not have the capital to acquire the property through more traditional methods. With MCC's 504 Loan Program, and their expertise and creative financing, I was able to satisfy the requirements for the down payment easily. MCC worked very hard on my behalf and made what could have been very difficult, a walk in the park. The entire staff at Mercantile is extremely knowledgeable with the entire loan process, making it streamlined from beginning to end. From funding construction draws to my general contractor, to acquiring more money toward the end of the construction process, they were there for me every step of the way. Their customer service is fantastic. When my initial engineer wasn't working out for me, they provided me with a referral to an engineer that made things much easier. I would definitely choose a SmartChoice® loan again and I would definitely use Mercantile Capital again. Mercantile Capital also worked around my schedule and took care of things while I was busy seeing patients. They understood I was busy running my business. I was able to handle everything in regard to my loan over the phone, with a weekly or bi-weekly phone call, when necessary. A couple of documents here or there were faxed to me for signatures, and I was rolling. I whole-heartedly recommend them to anyone who wishes to buy commercial real estate."

Dr. Ben Larson, O.D., Owner
Advanced EyeCare of Central Florida
Sanford, FL
advancedeyecareflorida.com

"Mercantile is playing an essential and valuable role in the encouragement of superior educational opportunities for our young people. This new loan will enable the school to expand in numbers and invest in additional well-qualified staff. It also facilitates development of the infrastructure needed for this growth in the arts, technology, career and fitness components of the curriculum. I am grateful for the efficiency, thoroughness and personal attention that Mercantile gave to the loan process. They guided me through the requirements with great sensitivity to the unique business that a private high school represents, while

YOU CAN DO IT

holding it to the rigors of a business transaction. More than that, I felt that Mercantile was not merely providing a loan, but a validation of the importance of consolidating the future of American private school education within a secure financial construct. Having dealt with a myriad of banks and other financial institutions over the years, I can say that the experience with Mercantile was truly a rewarding one."

PHILIP CLARKE, President and Owner
Arroyo Pacific Academy
Arcadia, CA
arroyopacific.org

"Financing a project is like threading a needle – it takes a few stabs before you get it. Not so with Mercantile. I know what I wanted and what I needed in financing to purchase a 'dream' deal. The realtor who put it together told me about Mercantile. Threading the needle became a cinch. They know exactly how to package the financing and simplify the process until closing. I literally just put my signature on the dotted line and the building was mine."

CARLOS GIRALDO, President & Founder
Central Reservation Service Corp.
Maitland, Florida
crshotels.com

"Once again, it was a pleasure to work with MCC, and they saw this through right to the finish line in their usual professional and upbeat manner. This deal is important to Central Florida, as we will now be using our Orlando facility as a training hub not only for Maine, but for all our further facilities as we continue our expansion."

CIARAN MCARDLE, Co-Owner
XL Soccer World Saco, LLC
Orlando, FL and Saco, ME
xlsoccerworld.com

"It was almost impossible to find a lender for our project. All of the banks were pessimistic and closed-minded to doing any kind of business. But Mercantile Capital was open to fight for us, and they worked hard for us until we got it. Thank you so much to all the Mercantile team!"

> **GRACIELA BLANCO,** Owner
> Silver Sea Homes, Inc.
> Altamonte Springs, FL
> silverseahomes.com

"Mercantile Capital Corporation was very easy to work with, professional and helpful in simplifying our loan process. We look forward to seeing our completed project, thanks to their hard work and assistance. We would definitely recommend Mercantile Capital Corporation as a lender for any small business."

> **ROBERT COMMISSO,** Co-Owner
> TriCom Coatings, Inc.
> Phoenix, AZ
> tricomcoatings.com

"In this economic climate, many businesses are not able to get financing. We had a critical need to expand our Orlando office. I did not want to take any chances, and based on my previous experience with Mercantile, I knew the transaction would go through. I was not disappointed, and everything happened on schedule, within the original cost estimates."

> **HOWARD IKEN,** Owner
> The Divorce Center, P.A.
> Tampa, FL
> 18884mydivorce.com

"We had a great experience with Mercantile, and a very professional and timely closing."

> **DR. UMESH PATEL,** Co-Owner
> Roslyn Claremont Hotel
> Roslyn, NY
> roslynclaremonthotel.com

"Mercantile treated us like family and made the financing of our property for our business smooth and easy. We could not have asked for better service. MCC's staff was attentive, knowledgeable, and responsive to our every concern. They answered all of our questions quickly and professionally. I could not have asked for an easier process. We will continue to do business with Mercantile for any future lending needs and continue to recommend them to our friends for their next commercial real estate purchases."

Mario Costa, VP of Operations
Infinite Personal Possibilities, Inc.
Aventura, FL
ipp.cc

"Our first motivation was that it's an investment type of move – we wanted to own versus rent, but we also needed to expand because our patient population had expanded. This program turned out to be excellent. It happened so easily that I'm amazed."

Dr. Burgos, Owner
Family Physicians of BVL
Kissimmee, FL
fpg-florida.com

"In evaluating my options for financing, I decided to use SBA financing primarily for the low upfront cash injection. With SBA financing, we are able to keep that additional money in the company to assist with our growth. When I took a look at my options for lenders, Mercantile Capital Corporation came highly recommended."

Richard Bodwell, President & CEO
Innovative Service Solutions
Orlando, FL
innovativeservicesolutions.com

"Working with Mercantile was great. Not only did they have excellent product knowledge, but they were available well past regular working hours, which was so helpful, considering we still had a business to run during the loan process."

Michael & Arden Cottle, Co-Owners
Out-Spoke'N Bike Shops, Inc.
Lake Mary, FL
outspokenbikes.com

"I worked with several Central Florida Banks over a four month time period. None of the Banks were able to deliver the necessary financing. Mercantile Capital had a commitment in three weeks and the loan closed five weeks later. They handled the entire process in a very professional, expeditious manner."

> **BILL BERG,** Owner
> National Cylinder Services, LLC
> Orlando, FL
> natcyl.com

"Purchasing our school building was an enjoyable transaction with Mercantile. Their team was organized and not only were the forms and documents requested in a precise fashion, but they were not overwhelming. The specific requirements of our childcare business were treated as top priority, and MCC was knowledgeable in these matters. I look forward to the day I call them, and tell them I'm ready to purchase my next facility."

> **KIM BARNES,** Owner
> Academic Beginnings Childcare, LLC
> Sanford, FL
> academicbeginningschildcare.com

"When I got ready to purchase my office building in College Park, I assumed, as a female small business owner, that it would be difficult obtaining a commercial loan with reasonable terms at a good interest rate. After shopping around, my real estate broker lead me to Mercantile Capital Corporation. After clearly explaining which loan would be best for my business circumstances, they went above and beyond, processing applications and staying on top of the entire loan process during the busy '05 holiday season. In fact, we were filing papers the day before and day after Christmas! We closed on Monday, January 9. They could not have been more helpful, nor could they have been more professional."

> **KIMBRA HENNESSY,** Partner
> Bitner Goodman
> Orlando, FL
> bitnergoodman.com

"MCC is a team of professionals. Buying commercial property for the first time is a HUGE step – not to mention scary. MCC made us feel comfortable and at ease the moment we walked in their office. From then on, it was smooth sailing. We look forward to working with them again in the future."

TAMERA DUNCAN, Co-Owner
Laser Line, Inc.
Casselberry, FL

"Chris has a tremendous talent for listening to and communicating with people. Unlike any other loan experience, either business or personal, Chris actually made the process almost seem enjoyable."

TIM SAUNDERS, President and Owner
Lasereliance Technologies
Longwood, FL
lasereliance.com

"Chris is one of the few people who do what they say and do it when they say they will. He knows the industry specs to the letter. As a business owner I expect service, value and follow through, and Chris does all of the above. A rare find!"

MILLIE CRENSHAW, President and Owner
Southern Title & Abstract
Orlando, FL
southerntitle-abstract.com

Build Your Team Wisely

Because SmartChoice® Commercial Loans (aka SBA 504 loans) have many moving parts, getting everything and everyone in sync can sometimes be a challenge. This is why it's important to do your homework up front, as I discussed earlier, and choose the right people to work with for your unique project. I've included the following comments from some advisors (real estate brokers, mortgage brokers, general contractors, CDCs, and so on) as examples of things you should look for from others you're thinking about working with. Here's what small business advisors have said about Mercantile:

....

"If I were to choose one word to describe my experience working with Mercantile it would be speed. They are extremely quick and proficient. Most of the time, we are used to stepping in and handling everything. We usually end up going a step further with the buyer and handle a lot of the negotiations with the lender. We haven't had to do that with the two recent deals that we've completed with Mercantile. From the very beginning, we understood their parameters, and that's important for us when trying to sell a piece of real estate. We've gone to [potential buyers], stood there on-sight with a calculator and said, 'You need to put approximately 10% down. This is approximately going to be your rate. Call these guys.' Mercantile had a very clear understanding up front with us – standing on-site while looking at the property – of what their monthly debt service was going to be and how that compared to paying rent. Mercantile has done a great thing in making this a painless process for us and doing it in a very timely manner. They kept up with the contracts' critical dates extremely well."

BILLY BISHOP, Principal
BishopBeale
Orlando, FL
bishopbeale.com

"Most people, when you mention the SBA, get wide-eyed and they immediately think of piles of paperwork. I always tell them about the advantages of the 504 that I'm aware of and then tell them to call Chris [Hurn] because he can explain it much better than I can – he's an expert and this is all these guys do. If you ask me about SBA loans, I will say that you have to go through Mercantile. There are other banks out there that say they can do a 504 loan, but if they don't do it that often, you're probably headed for one of the stereotypical SBA experiences with lots of paperwork and hassles. The 504 loan is a perfect fit for most small and mid-sized businesses looking to buy commercial real estate. I know that the program definitely has its advantages, and I would rather somebody talk to Chris and hear it from an expert at 504 loans."

RAY ROMANO, First Vice President
CBRE
Orlando, FL
cbre.us

"I would say that Mercantile gave us a level of comfort that I haven't found anywhere else, so I always give Chris the first opportunity when I have a deal that's 504-eligible. There have been loans that I didn't think Chris could even help us with – one of them was a Marina in South Florida, but it turned out they helped us close that loan. To me, that deal goes to show the flexibility that Chris and everyone has at Mercantile to help us get loans done. So, regardless of the situation, I let him have the first shot as often as I can on everything we do. What's cool about the guys and gals at Mercantile is they are always willing to talk to the client. They understand that I am a broker, and they don't want me to be out of the loop on anything, so they allow me to keep my involvement in the deal. Some banks don't really want you talking to the client after they get a hold of them; whereas Chris will let me just do whatever I need to do for my client. If I have questions, he is always willing to meet with people and explain things, which always helps. And Geof provides a wealth of knowledge – he's wise, brilliant. Everybody at Mercantile has been good to us. We've built a great relationship. It's a long-lasting relationship. It's comforting to know that we can always send deals to them. Anybody that has the opportunity to do business with Mercantile, I highly recommend it. Everything Mercantile does is cutting-edge and super creative, in both marketing and finance. They are like rock stars in the world of small business lending!"

STEVE & DITA ROBINSON, Owners
Countrywide Commercial Mortgage Brokers, Inc.
Bradenton, FL

"It's a pleasure to work with Mercantile, and especially Chris, because he knows the ins and outs of the small business loan process. He has a lot of experience, and he has the ability to make a once-tedious process as easy as getting a conventional loan. A client of mine who worked with Mercantile had never owned anything before I hooked him up with them. He had always rented. Now he's calling me looking for other investment opportunities in real estate. But that's typical. I can't tell you any person that I've ever been involved with as a tenant before they owned, that ever went back to leasing again. And if they're using it for their own business operation, they need to do it with Mercantile's financing because it keeps their capital available. It's the greatest leverage still out there for a small business."

MICHAEL HEIDRICH, Principal
NAI Realvest
Maitland, FL
realvest.com

"Mercantile's team had the expertise to understand the financial data for this specialty industry and to see the strong potential of this investment. Their application process was smooth, the appraisal was handled quickly and competently, the loan documents were ready for review when promised, closing took place on time and with obvious professionalism. I help investors in the field of child daycare across the U.S., and I've worked with a lot of banks. I am impressed with the service Mercantile provided, and I will look forward to working with them again."

DR. BEN STAFFORD, Owner
Day Care Franchise Consultant
Beaumont, TX
daycarefranchise.com

"We appreciate our relationship with Mercantile. The staff is professional, knowledgeable of the program and quick to respond to every issue or inquiry.

Not only has our CDC been pleased with your program and people, but our borrowers have also. We have received nothing but compliments on your application process and turnaround time. It is a pleasure working with Mercantile and we hope to work with them on many other projects in the future."

> **JOHN HART**, President
> East Texas Regional Development Company
> Kilgore, TX
> etrdc.com

"I recently closed my first transaction with Mercantile. I submitted the file with a lot of fear as my relationship with the customer was on the line. The loan officer for this deal quickly issued a commitment letter, and continued to provide help as turbulence bounced us through the transaction. I am thankful I had the Mercantile team to help resolve issues and see through the hundreds of details in the transaction. No crash and burn here. I will continue to send my business to Mercantile."

> **RYAN GOLDACKER**, President
> Legacy Lending Group, Inc.
> Fort Wayne, IN
> legacylending.biz

"In working through a transaction brought to us by Mercantile, I found both Chris and his organization to be very professional. The loan package they sent me was thorough and complete. Both Chris and his organization were very knowledgeable of the 504 program and when issues arose, Chris demonstrated his flexibility in bringing this transaction to a conclusion. It would be my pleasure to have the opportunity to work with Chris and his organization on another 504 transaction in the future."

> **IRA P. LUTSKY**, President
> New Jersey Business Finance Corp.
> Fort Lee, NJ

"We recently worked with Chris on a project here in Iowa and without his support and assistance, the project would not have happened. Although located in Florida, Chris responded to our clients' far away call for assistance and based upon both his knowledge and commitment to the SBA 504 Loan Program, elected to assist the small business in its third business endeavor here in Iowa. We, as the CDC in the project, are very appreciative of his efforts and commitment to the program."

STEPHEN A. BRUSTKERN, Executive Director
Black Hawk Economic Development, Inc.
Waterloo, IA
bhed.org

"Freedman & Michaels represented a client who used Mercantile Capital Corporation to finance their acquisition of a business property on Florida's west coast. My client had significant deadline constraints, and I have never seen a lender mobilize so many professionals, within 24 hours, to meet a last minute closing deadline. They were quick, competent and professional, and I would eagerly recommend them to anyone needing commercial property financing."

LINDA M. MICHAELS, Partner
Freedman & Michaels
Tampa, FL

"Mercantile Capital Corporation and Chris Hurn have exceeded my expectations with conduct above reproach. They have displayed an earnest desire to put their customers' needs above their own. Loan commitments and loan closings are expedited and executed on time. Integrity and professionalism are alive and well at Mercantile. The nicest thing about working with them is the fact that they make the process look simple. So many horror stories are out there about working with the SBA that there is a natural reluctance a person has to do it. But, once I've been able to introduce the customer to Mercantile and they spend a short period of time with them, they take what is a complex process – they've done it so many times – and they make it look simple. They put business owners at ease with their qualifications and their abilities and they make it possible for my customers to fulfill dreams and do things that they didn't think they'd be able to do. Working with Mercantile, from a general contractor's perspective, it's been a good relationship. They have been very straightforward. If it's something that they can do, they jump on it. They get it done with enthusiasm – it's done. And if it's something they can't do, rather than beating around the bush, they just say, 'Charles it's not something we can do,' which is fine. I like everything on the table and that's the way these guys play. They play everything right on the table. Decisions are made and we move on. So I've had a great experience with

Mercantile as a contractor. Mercantile is different in that they are businessmen themselves and that makes all the difference in the world. When they look at a deal, they are looking at it through the eyes of the businessman. They're not looking at it through the eyes of the banker or through the eyes of an attorney (as far as whether something's legal or not). A lot of things are legal, but they're terrible business decisions. They're businessmen and that makes all the difference in how they approach a deal."

> **CHARLES EDWARDS**, President
> The Gainesborough Group, Inc.
> Orlando, FL
> gainsboroughgroup.com

"Thank you for taking such good care of my client and friend. The closing was one of the most informative and best-explained closings I've been to in years. I know my client has felt confident with your company from the very first phone call and with each individual from that point forward."

> **SHIRLEY WELCH**, Realtor
> Watson Realty Corp.
> Orlando, FL
> watsonrealtycorp.com

"I have closed SBA loan transactions for many years and for many lenders. This gives me the experience and ability to say that Mercantile is among the most prepared and best lenders with whom I have worked. They excel at being responsive; a quality we emphasize at my law firm, and one that all of us appreciate. Mercantile's 504 loan program is handled by professionals who know what they are doing, and they do it well. Mercantile is easy to work with, and they do whatever they can to make each borrower's loan experience an excellent one. That is why they are one of the fastest growing lenders in the 504 loan market in the U.S."

> **MITCHELL C. FOGEL**, Principal and Founder
> Fogel Law Group
> Boca Raton, FL
> fogellawgroup.com

"Thankfully, with the overall low cost of capital and leverage flexibility that the SBA 504 Loan Refinance Program provides, we were able to prevent a possible foreclosure while significantly reducing our client's overall borrowing costs."

JOEL NATHANSON, Broker
ACG Companies
Irvine, CA
acgcompanies.com

Acknowledgements
and Gratitude

First, a big "THANKS" to the folks who regularly follow my blog (www.504Blog.com) and who provided the title for this book, as well as helped me choose the cover design. Yes, we "crowdsourced" it, and you have my apologies if yours was one of the over 1,300 possible titles submitted that did not get the most votes – over 2,900 votes came in as well. Thank you so much for your enthusiasm and support.

Thanks to my lovely wife, Shannon, who put up with one too many, "I've got to work on my book tonight," comments. I'm still awe-struck by your love and support 21 years after having laid eyes on you.

Thank you, Mom, for being such an entrepreneurial inspiration. I'm sure you didn't even know it at the time, but the impression it has left on me was and is profound. In many ways, I'm glad we had all of our struggles and hardships in the past because it has made us truly appreciate more of what we have today.

Thank you, Geof. You've been the best business partner a guy could ask for. Kinda shocking that all these years later you're not the only "gray hair" anymore. Thanks for taking a chance on a 29-year-old kid when you did. I think things have worked out pretty well.

Over the years, I've had numerous mentors and inspirers, some I've known personally, while others taught me from afar: from books, audio tapes, CDs, videos, lectures, and so on. To those folks I must also say a big "THANK YOU" and mention a few, in no particular order, that come to mind at this moment: Gordon "Gordie" Wassell; Dr. Jay "Doc" Williams; Annie Baran; Victor Frankl; Milton Friedman; Dr. Jim Spady; Jamie Humes; Tom Peters; Ayn Rand; Peter Drucker; Jay Abraham; Robert Kiyosaki; Joseph Schumpeter; Dan Kennedy (*and also for your book endorsement*); Jim Collins; Robert Ringer; Napoleon Hill; Robert Cialdini; George Gilder; Gene Simmons; Jim Rohn; Shelby Steele; Bo Burlingham (*and also for your book endorsement*); Stuart Wilde; F.A. Hayek; Gene Landrum; Hugh MacLeod; Eric Hoffer; Felix Dennis; Ram Charan; Elon Musk; Brian Wesbury; Tim Ferriss; Dinesh D'Souza; Peter Thiel; Robert Greene; Donny Deutsch; Guy Kawasaki; Tony Hsieh; Michael Lewis; and Neil Strauss (*and also for your sage book advice*). Many of these people have books that should be on your nightstand, if not in your library.

I've also had the great pleasure of masterminding and networking with some of the best minds in business today. To these folks, I bid you a hardy "THANK YOU" for your ideas, suggestions and inspiration over the years (*again, in no particular order*): Andrew Lock; Dr. Charley Martin; Perry Marshall; Victor Cheng; Bill Harrison; Frank Kern; Rory Fatt; Bill Hammond; Stephen Oliver; Dave Dee; Jimmy (Vee) and Travis (Miller) (*and also for your book endorsement*); Yanik Silver; Stephen Snyder; Chris Tomshack (*and also for your book endorsement*); Rob Berkley (*and also for your book endorsement*); Darin Garman; Robert Skrob; Robert Miller; Brian Fricke; Michael Cage; Jon Keel; Rob Minton; Mike Midget; Ron Ipach; Richelle Shaw; Bob Campana; Scott Tucker; Nigel Worrall; my YPO Forum Brothers; and my Society Brothers.

THANK YOU to all those who reviewed this book and wrote glowing endorsements (*and haven't already been mentioned*): T. Harv Eker; Jay Goltz; Norm Brodsky; Eric Abrahamson; Sally Hogshead; Bill Taylor; Sam Calagione; David Morey; Joseph Michelli; Bob Coleman (*and for prodding me to finish for several years*); and Ari Weinzweig.

I would be remiss if I didn't mention the great help I received from my friend and publisher, Adam Witty, as well as Bob Sheasley, my editor, and

Brooke White, as well as ALL of the others at Advantage. I have to mention a special thanks to Clint Greenleaf for being so honorable as well.

And last, but by no means least, I'm so very grateful to my entire team at Mercantile who make me look good daily, especially the "old-guard": Trey, Nikos, Robin, Tony, Kenneth, Dawn, Shannon, Sean, Dwayne, Angela, Dan, and Yelena. Truly, a guy couldn't ask for a more competent group of professionals. While we may not get to "pick" our families, I got to pick most of you, and I'm honored to have spent nearly a quarter of my life with you.

I would hope I haven't forgotten anyone, but I'm sure that's entirely probable. My apologies if I've forgotten to mention you by name. While this has been my side-project, I've always been honored and grateful for any help you've provided along my journey.

I confess that this book was about four years in the making. It kept getting pushed to the back burner as we grew Mercantile. I once heard that writing a book is like slitting your wrists with a rusty razor and letting the words pour out onto the page. I think I must have held onto that vivid description in my mind a bit too long. I actually *like* writing and have done a lot of it, but I always thought a book was a much larger undertaking. Now finished, it turns out it wasn't as difficult as I thought it would be. I've scaled this mountain. Now, I'm on to others.

I hope you've found this book educational, entertaining, and inspirational. Now go create some wealth for yourself and the betterment of the world!

Investing in Our Future

The role of small businesses in America's economy is huge, and today's students are tomorrow's entrepreneurs and business owners. Unfortunately, entrepreneurship is something that's rarely taught in the classroom (though, it's happening more often than it used to). The National Federation of Independent Business (NFIB) is one of the more powerful to represent small businesses in America, and their Young Entrepreneur Foundation (YEF) is doing great things to help students learn about the critical role of small business in the American free enterprise system.

The NFIB YEF primarily works to identify students who are interested in small business and entrepreneurship, and helps to further their education in the form of scholarships and awards. Because we think entrepreneurship is such a great thing for young people to learn and become excited about – and because entrepreneurship will continue to drive innovation and grow our economy – we're investing in the NFIB YEF in the following way:

When you buy two or more copies of this book (say, one for you and one you give to a friend), we'll donate the net proceeds of the sale to the NFIB YEF. All we need is a copy of your receipt showing the purchase, and that can be emailed (info@mercantilecc.com), faxed (407-682-1632) or mailed (60 N. Court Avenue, Suite 200, Orlando, FL 32801).

Thanks for your interest in this book, and for helping us help young entrepreneurs further their education, our economy of tomorrow, and all of our chances for success.

CPSIA information can be obtained at www.ICGtesting.com
Printed in the USA
LVOW082141010513

331919LV00006B/186/P